ELEVATE YOUR MINDSET

ELEVATE YOUR MINDSET

THE MOST INSPIRING WAY TO TAKE YOUR MINDSET TO THE NEXT LEVEL

Foreword by Dr John Demartini
Human Behaviour Specialist, Educator & Teacher From 'The Secret'

Disclaimer

All the information, techniques, skills and concepts contained within this publication are of the nature of general comment only and are not in any way recommended as individual advice. The intent is to offer a variety of information to provide a wider range of choices now and in the future, recognising that we all have widely diverse circumstances and viewpoints.

Should any reader choose to make use of the information contained herein, this is their decision, and the contributors (and their companies), authors and publishers do not assume any responsibilities whatsoever under any condition or circumstances. It is recommended that the reader obtain their own independent advice.

First Edition 2018

Copyright © 2018 by Author Express

All rights reserved. No part of this publication may be reproduced, stored in a retrieval system, or transmitted in any form or by any means, electronic, mechanical, photocopying, recording or otherwise, without the prior written permission from the publisher.

National Library of Australia
Cataloguing-in-Publication entry:

Title: Elevate Your Mindset
ISBN(s): 9781925471328
Series: Elevate Books

Creator: Harvey, Benjamin J., author.
Other Authors:
Altuney, Aldwyn |Bliss, Peter |Duque, Patty, |Farrow, Cherry |Fox, Rebecca| Freeman, Elissa |Jackson, Shirley Jane | Kudhal, Rani| Laing, Sharon

 A catalogue record for this book is available from the National Library of Australia

Published by Author Express
www.AuthorExpress.com
publish@authorexpress.com

Dedication

To fellow learners wanting to take their mindset to the next level. This book is dedicated to you.

Benjamin J Harvey and co-authors

Foreword by Dr John Demartini

When I was just 17 years old, I met an inspiring elderly man named Paul C. Bragg who changed my life. He did it by drawing out of me a profound and inspiring vision of my destiny that elevated my true worth and transformed my beliefs about what was possible for me. He taught me that when you can see it, you can be it. That extraordinary man gave me the affirmation, "I am a genius and I apply my wisdom" and told me to say it every day for the rest of my life. Even though I was just a near-illiterate young surfer at the time, I trusted him and followed his guidance diligently. I've never missed a day of saying that affirmation in more than 45 years and I know it's one of the major reasons why I am where I am and who I am now.

What you believe about and what you say to yourself will have a tremendous impact on what happens to you and what kind of life you'll lead. You are the creator of your own destiny. You write the script of your life with every thought. The more self-worth and love you have for yourself, the more prosperity and success you will achieve.

You are wise to have a mindset that believes you have something to offer in each area of your life. Owning the fact that you are valuable is an essential mindset and strategy.

Everyone lives by a set of values, from most important to least important. Your highest values are those you're inspired from within to do spontaneously. As you move down your list of priorities, you require outside motivation to do it. When you set a goal that's aligned to your highest values, you will experience increased confidence, achievement and belief, and will therefore experience more success.

The secret to success is learning to serve, shifting your mindset from what can I get, to what can I also give or contribute. When you help enough people get what they want, you truly make a difference. And if you're grateful for being able to serve, then you, too, will get what you want.

Start to get clear about what is really important to you. Start to clarify what you really want to go after. Then structure your life and take action on things that are really important and meaningful to you. When you do, you won't beat yourself up and think that you are having problems with achievement. Realise that you are an achiever. We all are, in our highest values, achievers. So make sure that you set goals that are really meaningful to you.

When the voice and vision on the inside become more profound and clearer than the opinions on the outside, then you have mastered your life.

Dr John F. Demartini
Human Behaviour Specialist
www.DrDemartini.com

BONUS GIFT

The Elevate YOU
7 Day Transformation

Want to take the top 7 areas of your life to the next level?

There is ONE powerful 'Elevate Process' you can use immediately to improve Your Relationships, Health, Finances, Mindset and any other area of your life.

In this transformational 7 day online course, Benjamin J Harvey guides you through the 'Elevate Process' and how you can improve your life from the inside-out.

**Normally valued at $295
Get FREE and instant access here:**

www.elevatebooks.com/you

Life Rewards Action. Get started today!

Contents

Myelin and Mindset   1
Benjamin J Harvey

Harness Your Happiness   41
Patty Duque

Mind Fitness   63
Rani Kudhal

Mindfulness   85
Peter Bliss

Mindset and Meaning   103
Rebecca Fox

Your Best Self   123
Cherry Farrow

Know Thyself   141
Sharon Laing

A Creative Mind   161
Elissa Freeman

Mindset and Wellness   181
Shirley Jane Jackson

Inspiring Good News   197
Aldwyn Altuney

"Giving yourself permission
to do what you love is the key to
elevating all areas of your life."

~ Benjamin J Harvey

Benjamin J Harvey

Myelin and Mindset

In his pursuit to assist people in finding the answers to life's most intriguing questions, Benjamin J Harvey has studied the psychology of empowerment for over ten years. Knowing that reading books like the Elevate series empowers people to bring their dreams into reality, Benjamin has been assisting thousands of people across the globe to empower themselves and live abundantly on purpose.

In 2009 he founded Authentic Education with business partner Cham Tang, to help people live a rich life. As a result, Authentic Education went on to achieve something that has never been done before in the history of personal development. They received the BRW Fast Starters Award in 2013 and then backed it up in 2015 by being named in the BRW Fast 100 as the thirty-eighth fastest-growing company in Australia.

Benjamin J Harvey
Myelin and Mindset

What is Mindset?

Mindset is defined as an attitude, disposition or mood, but I think it comes down to a set of rules you create to either live the life of your dreams...or not. These rules determine the choices you make, and those choices form your results. If you want to change your results, you first must change the rules you live by.

Your mindset is the very thing that shapes your world through beliefs, assumptions and philosophy of life. It can stop or empower you, so examining all aspects of it is crucial to experiencing the life you want to live.

Mindset is critical in acquiring a loving relationship, having the body you want, enjoying fulfilling holidays, having financial freedom and bringing success into your life, but the unfortunate fact is that it's underappreciated and underutilised.

One of my passions in life is to help people live the life that they love, experience the fulfillment they desire and to spend even more time with their loved ones. This all becomes possible with mindset and action. In every program Authentic Education creates, mindset and understanding how neurons factor into it, is a huge component.

Your education starts with our Turning Point Intensive free event we offer to give back to the community, where the core theme is simply, "Life Rewards Action".

Is it possible to change someone's mindset?

Yes, absolutely, as long as the person is open to change, is willing to look at situations differently and is ready to do whatever it takes to alter their life.

It isn't hard to change someone's mindset. A really good advertisement that shows a different way of looking at a situation can cause a small mindset change. This is why it's important to use caution with what you put into your mind. You're being influenced all of the time by everything around you, both covertly and overtly, and it's time you had a good hard look at what you're infusing into your mind, as it's producing the results you achieve and receive in life.

What do you think stops people from creating change in their life?

I've been helping people create strategies and transformation in their life for ten years with both my coaching business and Authentic Education's PHD programs, and over that time I've discovered there are three core issues people come up against when they want to create some change in their life.

1. **Not taking the time to automate their success.**

   The best of the best have a system for automating their success, but people rarely take time out of their life to work on it. You may have heard the saying, "You need to work *on* your business, not *in* your business." The same goes for life. But after thousands of hours of working with people, I can attest they continue to do tasks that could easily be automated. This means they're still doing a lot of unnecessary heavy lifting.

   People might crave a greater level of self-love, but the fact is, if they don't have time to do what they love, how could they ever expect it to occur? They're burning through their time, so by the end of the week, they have none left to do what they love, and then they wonder why they don't truly love themselves. It's a chicken and egg thing.

2. **An unwillingness to learn how to become their own best coach.**

There are systems that can help with mindset and emotional issues, such as anxiety and depression, that will create a healthy mind-body connection, so you can have a more fulfilling life.

However, nobody is taught these systems at any point in time, so they have to go and educate themselves outside the general education system. But people aren't willing to learn how to be their own best healer, and as a result they spend decades battling with issues inside of their mind and body, dealing with emotional traumas and significant events they don't know what to do with years later. They don't realise that if they'd just taken a couple of days out to learn how to self-heal, they'd be able to fix these issues.

3. **Not taking the time to learn the way of the wealthy.**

A person can spend tons of time and money fixing their mindset, relationships, health, career, connection with family and fitness, but if they neglect one specific area, it can unravel everything else. Some may think it's self-love, or emotions, or worthiness, but it's none of these.

That area is...wealth. Now unfortunately, a lot of people walk around saying, "Money's not important. It doesn't matter. It doesn't have any relevance." But if you trace back the origins of wealth back thousands of years, you'll discover that whoever was the wealthiest was also the healthiest.

Most people become stressed out and have arguments about money with loved ones, so it creates stress. And most studies regarding stress, state that it's the origin of almost every major catastrophic disease in the body. Therefore, it's safe to say that money does impact your health, because of the stress it creates.

So you can fix up your relationship until it's the best ever, but if you're flat broke, been kicked out of your home and have to sleep on the street with your partner, that relationship isn't going to survive.

Or let's just say you get your career sorted, but you can't afford to ever go on holidays, because you don't make enough, even though you're always working. You also have no time to devote to relationships or family, which creates huge amounts of stress.

When your self-worth goes up, your net worth goes up in correlation. You need to take the time to learn the way of the wealthy. In doing so, you'll allow all of the other areas to be sustained, because although money doesn't make you happy, it does provide options, and those options can bring happiness.

What role do neurons play in brain function?

Basically, a neuron is a thinking cell. They're designed to last a lifetime in the majority of the brain, and it was originally thought that if you killed one off, you didn't get it back.

But neurons have recently been proven to regenerate in certain areas of the brain by a process called *Neurogenesis*. Little is known about this phenomenon, and research is still being conducted.

These neurons, or thinking cells, are inside of your mind and body, and they allow you to compute ideas and information. If you want to pick up a pencil, the message would have to travel down a whole bunch of neurons and activate all different regions of your mind and body for you to pick it up. A child starts out incapable of getting a cup of water to their mouth, but over time, the precision gets clearer and clearer, until they can get the cup to the exact tilt angle with precision.

That precision is thanks to neurons wiring together and learning how to get the signals to happen at an exact moment in time. The more precision you have with the firing of neurons, the more accurate your behaviours become. It just takes a little time.

Inside of your neurons is this pure light, transmitting in the form of an electrical impulse. Now, if you have a hundred-billion neurons, keep in mind that each one can connect with as many as 10,000 other neurons, which means each one can go in 10,000 different directions. And there are as many as one-thousand-trillion synaptic connections.

So if you think you can't learn something new, think again, because you have one-thousand-trillion different connections, which is just shy of the number of grains of sand on planet Earth.

This means people are chemical and electrical in nature. The computer inside your head is quite powerful. To put things in perspective, nineteen-million volumes of encyclopaedias only adds up to 10,000 terabytes, and you have anywhere from a ten to one-hundred terabyte memory. So while your memory may not be infinite, you will never be able to fill it, because the human memory fades and rewrites itself over time.

But what does this have to do with creating a turning point? The good news is that a neuron rewires itself in about two seconds, so you can change your life that quickly.

But here's the bad news: you can also change it back in two seconds. You've heard the saying that old habits are hard to break? Change is easy. Changing back is just as easy.

So how can someone use this knowledge to produce results in their life?

Even though neurons have received a lot of publicity and are quite famous in the neuroscience world, they're not really what you want to research. In fact, it's not even that interesting anymore. But unfortunately, when neurons were discovered, the scientific world pushed aside some major research they were working on and jumped on the neurons.

This means we're decades, if not centuries, behind what we should have been researching.

In the sixteenth century, Andreas Vesalius discovered white matter. Until then, people believed the brain was only made up of grey matter.

But it wasn't until 1854 that Rudolf Virchow, a German pathologist, physician, scientist, pre-historian and author, decided to identify this white matter for the first time ever. He named it after the Greek word *milos*, which stands for marrow, and created the word *myosin*, or what's now referred to as myelin.

Once advancements were achieved regarding neurons, people blankly decided myelin was just this thing that insulated the neurons, and they stopped researching it, which is unfortunate, because myelin matters more than anything else. It's what produces actual results.

Most neurons consist of three distinct regions: the cell body (or soma), with branching dendrites (receivers) and the axon (which transmits information away from the cell body).

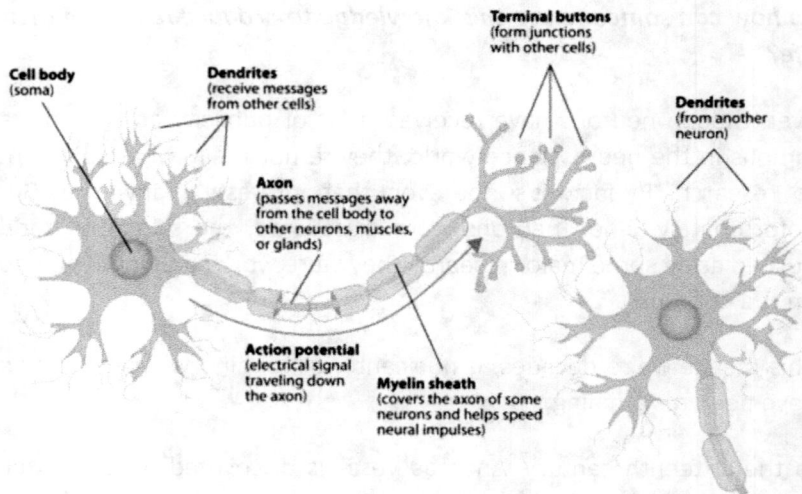

In the science world, the study of myelin was pushed aside, because they believed it was excreted out of the axon, or, in essence, that it wraps and insulates itself. But in 1954, it was discovered that myelin isn't excreted out of the axon. It's actually wrapped onto the axon by glial cells, which in regards to the peripheral nervous system is called a Schwann cell.

All axons in the peripheral nervous system are surrounded by Schwann cells, and the cover produced by these cells is often referred to as the sheath of Schwann.

Schwann cells that surround large diameter axons undergo a wrapping process called myelination. It begins when one part of the Schwann cell moves along the surface of the axon, and the leading edge slides underneath the outer portion of the Schwann cell, pushing it out of the way.

Once the myelination process completes, the cell is myelinated, which means the Schwann cell has covered the axon with many layers of plasma membranes consisting of eighty percent lipids and twenty percent protein, known as the myelin sheath.

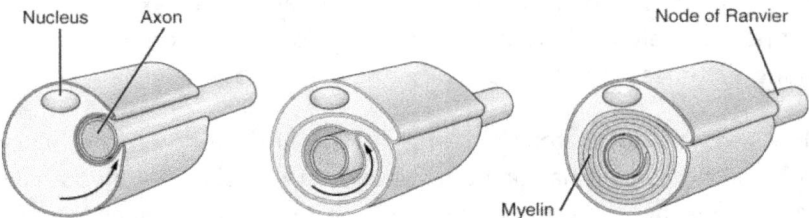

A neuron typically has one axon that connects it with other neurons, or with muscle or gland cells. Some axons can reach from the spinal cord down to a toe. The myelin sheath increases the speed of impulse transmission because the nerve impulse jumps from node to node. The reason this process is important is because the sheath not only insulates the cell, but it allows for precision of activity to occur at a single point.

In 1977, the first-ever magnetic resonance imaging scan was created with an MRI machine, which meant being able to view head traumas noninvasively. This was a major advancement in technology.

In 1985, the diffusion weighted image (DWI), was developed. This is where the MRI machine works out how to observe the diffusion of liquid inside the image.

In 1996 there came the diffusion tensor image (DTI), and for the first time in history, observation of myelin growing around a neuron became possible.

Now, how does this help with rewiring your brain? Well, the more you attempt a new task or way of thinking, the more you keep wrapping myelin around the axon, which means the information can travel faster down that neuron.

In terms of the speed difference, if you can get an axon wrapped proportionately to the diameter of the axon, that axon will travel a hundred times faster than any other neuron in your head.

The way this correlates to having a great life, sitting on the beach making money and hanging out with your friends, is that if you have your axons myelinating correctly, you will get to the destination point of your thinking, actions and behaviours a hundred times faster than the person next to you.

Let me give you a more practical example. If you were playing tennis against a professional and hit a ball to them, by the time they've worked out how they're going to whack it back, it would have taken you a hundred times longer to work it out. In essence, they have the shot ready to go a hundred times quicker than you do. So if it takes them one second to line up their shot, it would take you over a minute and a half before you were even close to being ready.

To myelinate a new road effectively, practise one action over and over again until it becomes unconscious competence. If you wanted to myelinate the perfect tennis serve, you would practice drawing the tennis racket back over and over, until you had the perfect angle. Just that one action, over and over again. If you make an error, stop, reset and start again. Then once you have the serve perfected, you move on to the next step, which would be throwing the ball up in the air over and over, until it produces the exact same result. You go through this for each piece in the serve, until they're perfected, and then you put it all together. This practical step-by-step action myelinates the roads to the perfect tennis serve. It's as simple as that. But people aren't taught this way.

When you myelinate the roads you want, you end up at your destination much faster, which means the actions you take are a hundred times faster with a hundred times more precision, and you get to where you want in life a lot quicker.

How does this relate to forming new habits?

What I'm getting across to you is the concept that at the end of the day, it's not about the neurons, it's about how you insulate them that's important. The more you're able to insulate the ones you want, the easier it becomes.

Many people in my industry believe that if you change your neurons, you change your wiring, and your traumas vanish. But myelin wraps, it doesn't unwrap, unless you're in the 0.000001% of the human race who has a major degenerative neurological illness. This means behaviours related to traumas you experienced when you were a kid still exist inside your mind. Now while you may think this is bad news, it isn't, because if it doesn't unwrap, then all you have to do is wrap the ones you want and stop wrapping the ones you don't.

It's unfortunate that a lot of therapy out there gets you to continually wrap the roads that don't need further insulation. You can get wisdom from your past, but every time you go back to it, just know you're wrapping myelin around it. In the last five years, there have been advancements in transformational technologies where the therapist no longer asks, "Would you please tell me the origin of your experience?" This is because of the research surrounding myelin.

I do a lot of therapy where I go back and check my past to gain an understanding of the origins of my current situation, but I'm aware of exactly what I'm doing.

You speak to anybody who used to smoke and ask them, "How quickly could you light up a cigarette if you really wanted to?" "In the blink of an eye" is usually the answer, but because they've formed the new identity of "I'm not a smoker anymore", they don't. However, the roads where the smoking exists are going to be wrapped for the rest of their life.

People in the personal development industry don't want to tell you this, but I will, because if you know the truth, then you can work on getting past it.

There's a saying that goes, "It's not that we know so much, it's that we know so much that isn't so."

Warren Buffett said, "The chains of habit are so light, you can't feel them until they're so heavy you can't break them."

If you keep myelinating the stuff you don't want, the road gets easier to travel, but if you start myelinating the roads you do want to take, your life changes. Again, you can myelinate a new road in less than two seconds.

Myelin doesn't discriminate. All it responds to is what you ask it to wrap. And it knows this through urgent repetition. That's it. Anything you do urgently and repetitively, it wraps, and vice-versa.

Let's say you're going to Santorini and will spend a couple of weeks there.

During your trip, you're picking up the language. "Wow!" you say. "Look at me speaking Greek". But then five months later you try to remember what you learned, and all you have left are maybe a couple of words or phrases. That's it. This is because when you were in Greece, you were firing those neurons repetitively, which means you were myelinating them. Then when you got back, there was no longer a reason to go down those roads, so you just left them where they were, to the point you can barely even find them. They're still present, you just don't know where you put them.

For instance, you probably can't remember what you had for lunch last Tuesday. Do you know why? Because you didn't myelinate it. Finding a fifteen-year-old memory of a major event is easier, because thanks to the media, you've wrapped it again and again, so when you fire the idea, you find the thought.

How can people use myelinating to change their life?

If you want to change your life starting today, just myelinate what you want. That's it. This is what's called *results matter*, because anything you wrap in myelin gets you the results you want.

When people talk about manifesting, they're talking about myelin and the production of it. Now, the good news is that you can speed up and slow down the production of myelin.

There's a way to increase myelin by a thousand times faster than the person sitting next to you, so it will look to the naked eye like you're performing miracles. Again, it doesn't discriminate. It takes the pressure off, but it also gets rid of all your excuses.

What is the Triune Brain?

Back in 1960, a neuroscientist and physician named Paul D. MacLean put forth the idea of the Triune Brain complex. He hypothesized that your brain existed in three evolutionary phases.

1. **The R-complex or reptilian brain**

    MacLean said that humans have a brain in common with reptiles.

    The R-complex is what's referred to quite often as the hindbrain or the brainstem. So the reptilian brain does survival instinctual behaviours, like breathing and other bodily functions, as well as ritual and territorial style activities.

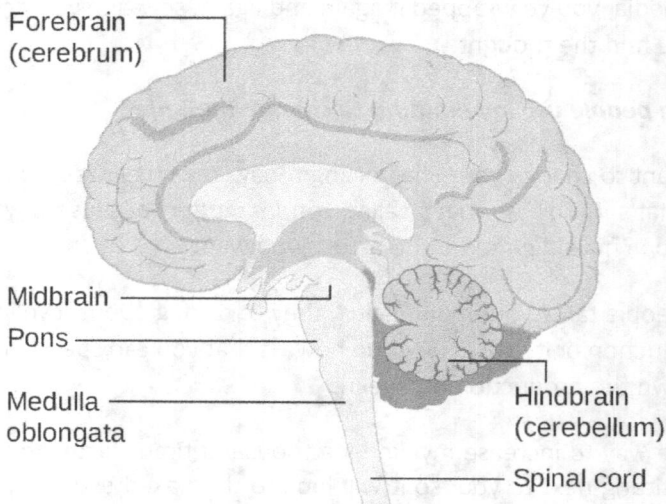

2. The Paleomammalian complex

From the R-complex you evolve into the Paleomammalian complex, which is from the Palaeolithic times. This is where you start to develop a conscious connective idea regarding reward centres and the ability to feel emotion and understand social cues.

3. Neomammalian complex

The Neomammalian complex is the latest addition and the most advanced piece of software, but it's actually the slowest technology you have in your brain.

It's responsible for language, planning, prioritisation, discernment, willpower and your ability to look in a mirror and recognise yourself.

So until this part of your brain was formed, you wouldn't have known who the heck was staring back at you in the mirror or be able to speak to people.

What are the roadblocks in the way of people getting what they desire?

Say you have a desire in your heart that you want to create something, whether it's a house by the beach or travelling the world or having a loving relationship. To get to your goal, you first have to get past the roadblocks on Myelin Road.

"YES TOWN"

Intelligence — Logic, planning, discernment and self-awareness

Imagination — Emotions, maps, social meaning, dreams & rewards

Instincts — Survival, breathing, heart rate, territorial & ritual behaviour

▶ **Checkpoint One: Instincts**

This is where your instincts will work out whether or not you're allowed to produce myelin. If your instincts say no, then no myelin will be produced, and you can't get to your goal.

Now, instincts are all about survival, such as heart rate, breathing, territory and ritual behaviour. At this checkpoint you're analysed from an instinctual perspective, and they're checking seven specific filters. Remember, if you don't get through checkpoint one, you don't make any myelin and get a hundred times faster. If someone can get their dream house in one day, it's going to take you a hundred days to get yours.

Here are the seven filters:

✓ **Filter one: Fear**

This is where your fear level is gauged regarding your goal. Now, you can create myelin when you have fear. There are a lot of people who experience it and still take action. It's been said that courage is not the absence of fear; it's getting through the fear, because what you want is much more important.

Removing fear isn't the essential element, but having something more important is, so it's about mitigation.

✓ **Filter two: Doubt**

How much doubt is there around what you're about to do? Are you feeling as if it's impossible? That you don't have the skills or stamina to make it happen?

✓ **Filter three: Danger**

There's usually a degree of danger in every major life change. Do you feel you can't combat those dangers? Do they seem like too much for you to handle?

- **Filter four: Suspicion**

    Suspicion creates doubt and mistrust. For instance, if you want to travel the world, you might be suspicious of meeting people who have different cultures and beliefs. Or maybe you have a suspicion that someone making a great offer is trying to swindle you.

- **Filter five: Boredom**

    If you think of doing something that bores you, you'll never start it. You can't myelinate it. If you get up to checkpoint one and say, "Hey, I want you to myelinate the most boring thing ever," it won't get insulated. The same goes for fear, doubt and danger. Your instincts won't allow you to myelinate any of these, because your instincts are saying, "Don't get better at boredom...Don't get better at fear...Don't get better at danger."

- **Filter six: Uncertainty**

    Your instincts don't want you to get better at uncertainty, because the more uncertainty you have in your life, the less-likely your reptilian brain can protect you from imminent danger.

    Your hindbrain loves repetition. It doesn't know what's good or bad. It just knows what didn't kill you. If yesterday you smoked twenty-five cigarettes and you didn't die, checkpoint one says, "Smoke 'em again, and don't smoke any fewer than that, because if you do, we could die!" This is why people repeat the most ridiculous behaviours that are absolutely detrimental to their long-term life experience. Filling your lungs with tar isn't the best thing for your lungs, but uncertainty isn't going to wrap that.

Checkpoint one only understands right now. This second. At most, a day.

- ✓ **Filter seven: Complication**

    Anything that's complicated won't be wrapped, because if it keeps wrapping more and more complex things, it won't know how to deal and protect you in a more complicated environment, so it likes to try and keep things as simple as possible.

These are the seven filters reviewed at checkpoint one before it makes the decision to myelinate anything.

Doubt often leads to fearing danger, so check for more than one filter at once, such as any uncertainty you're having about your goals.

If you wanted to write a book, you might doubt if anyone will buy it, which prevents the myelination from occurring. But just because you have these concerns, doesn't mean you can't move through them.

Checkpoint one is all about this concept of where your beliefs are formed. Everyone has beliefs that prevent them from moving forward in life, and a lot of checkpoint one is about them. If truth is that which never changes, then your beliefs can't be your truth, because they're transient.

As you travel around the world, your belief system gets destroyed, because what you absolutely think is the truth, you realise is just a belief. A lot of checkpoint one is your storage of beliefs that aren't real at all but are ones you think are helping you survive. They're not. They're limiting you from experiencing all that life has to offer.

▶ **Checkpoint Two: The realm of imagination.**

    This is where you store your emotions, maps, social meaning, dreams and rewards. In order to create myelin, you need to have a pre-existing imagination around what it is you want to create.

In your imagination, you have these maps around incidents that have shaped the way you view the world. If you leave the house with your imagination filled with exactly what they want, you'll see those opportunities. If not, you won't.

For instance, let's say you want to buy your dream house, but the only pictures in your imagination are of you trudging to a job every day you think is boring and lying in bed all day just tuning out and watching television.

If you get to checkpoint two without one image in your head of living in your dream home, you'll be stopped in your tracks, because this is where they scan for patterns.

The people who go out there and create an incredible level of myelin, achieve the most amazing results. They're the ones who spend hours and hours imagining the life they want. The whole world just becomes a breeze when you can understand myelin, because it doesn't care who you are. It just does its job when you activate it.

You have millions and billions of bits of information that are bombarding you all the time. In order for you to not get totally overwhelmed and have a nervous breakdown, your brain has a filtering process where it chunks that down to seven pieces of information. But when you become aware of one thing, you forget about the next, and so on.

The rule of thumb is seven, plus-or-minus two chunks, because that's how many you can handle at any given time and still feel okay. So from three billion down to seven, plus or minus two chunks, with 132 bits per chunk, which is a small amount of information.

All of these bits of information bombard your sense doors. They go through space, time, matter and energy before being filtered through your values language, memories, decisions and belief systems. Then you filter it through your attitude toward life, until all that's left is a small amount of information that lands on the screen of your mind's eye, which becomes your reality.

If you perceive that the whole world is filled with opportunity, then no matter what enters your senses, you'll filter it into the golden cup of opportunity, which affects your emotional state, physiology and behaviour. Then due to this filtering, you project this idea out into the world and see only opportunities everywhere you look. From there you can reach out and grab hold of it, and all of a sudden what you're projecting becomes the way you perceive the world.

Wayne Dyer, who was a mentor of mine, would often say that there are two types of people in the world: those who walk out of the house looking to be offended and those who see opportunity everywhere, and you have to decide which one you are.

Your reality is determined by your imagination and what you filter, which has a huge impact on the way you perceive the world.

▸ **Checkpoint Three: Intelligence**

This is about perception.

Intelligence is the realm of language, planning, prioritisation, discernment, willpower and self-awareness. It's also where you store different types of value systems.

If you can get yourself through all three checkpoints, you can get that myelin created. The whole idea behind the concept is to have all of them communicating in the same language.

You might feel like there are multiple types of communication going on inside your mind. For instance, you imagine having a beautiful car, but you're scared of someone scratching it, so you drive around in a beat-up clunker. Or every night you imagine having a loving partner, but you're petrified of being rejected, so instead you go to clubs on the weekends, get as drunk as possible, pass out and go home.

There are actually three conversations going on within you: your intelligence, your emotional state and your physiological actions (your mind, body and spirit). As you look more deeply, you'll discover that the secret to getting myelin to produce at the fastest level is to get all three of them to line up as one congruent conversation.

Why do people feel they need to get permission before they make a major change in their life?

Wayne Dyer believed we live in a permission-based reality.

But what does this mean?

When you first arrive on this planet, you're myelinating like crazy, and a lot of that myelination forms your imprint.

Because you've just myelinated stuff so thoroughly, it's almost impossible to break. In fact, psychologists and psychiatrists say that who you are as a person, meaning your personality type, traits, behaviours, distress patterns, and what makes you happy and sad, is set up before the age of five. That's how deep this myelin goes.

So as you go through the process, you're myelinating a lot of permission. May I go to the bathroom? May I stay up late? May I sit down?

What happens is that you myelinate the belief that you need permission from somebody else before you do anything in your own world. For instance, ninety-five percent of your behaviours surrounding money were set up before the age of ten, unless you've reprogrammed it, but very few people do.

Ask yourself who your influences were in regard to money, including your emotional state surrounding it. You'll probably be mortified to discover that the person who holds your bank account is younger than ten years of age, and their investment decisions are based around instant gratification.

I love the simplicity of everything Wayne Dyer taught. He said there were just two little words you needed to say over and over again: *I'm allowed*.

Go ahead and print them out on a sheet of paper and stick it inside your front door, so just before you leave the house you say, "I'm allowed."

Think about that. Wouldn't it be ridiculous to call up a friend to give them permission to do what they love? Of course, because it would be condescending. But believe it or not, people will continue along their path, until someone tells them it's okay to do something else. Of course, that's not going to happen.

However, that little imprinted myelinated section of your brain was fully set up with a permission idea. In fact, until you left home, you still had to get permission to do anything.

When achieving a goal, is it better to go it alone or with a team?

In regard to transformation, there's a Native American proverb that you go faster on your own, but further as a team.

If you follow through on your New Year's resolution and join a gym, the chances of you quitting is well above forty percent, as in not using it and giving up in a matter of three months. But if you join that gym with a friend, even if you don't work out on the same machines or take the same class together, your chance of cancelling your membership goes to less than five percent.

I'm a big fan of empowering your peer group and working out how to get the right people around you, because quite often those you hang around have a huge impact on what you do in life.

Everyone wants to be wealthy, but few people ever add someone who's wealthy to their peer group, and then listen to what they have to say about wealth. Or people who want to be happier don't go out of their way to add someone to their peer group who knows about emotions.

There's a saying that goes, "The safer you feel, the quicker you heal." Those you surround yourself with are there to make sure you have a safe and supportive environment in which to transform. That's why we created authentic.com.au for people all over the world to have access to the right support and peer groups.

How do people turn thoughts into action?

Many people believe imagination is all you need to turn thoughts into action. They saw the movie *The Secret*, so they sit at home just imagining what they want. And when ten years later nothing's changed in their lives, they say, "I followed everything the movie told me to do! I've been sitting on a milk crate in my house, imagining a Ferrari for years, but there's no Ferrari in my driveway!"

Unfortunately, *The Secret* left out a large chunk of the equation, known as action. There's a saying that goes, "If imagination was all it took, then every seven-year-old girl would have a pony." So, there's more to it than just imagination. It's having the right instincts, filters and level of intelligence, and using them in a precise action. If you get these three areas to work in conjunction, you can move mountains.

What is the success equation?

There's a successful entrepreneur named Kazuo Inamori, who's dubbed the Buddhist Billionaire. The reason he got this name is because he's Buddhist, and he built two multi-billion-dollar companies from nothing. He then rescued a third, Japanese Airways, which he also turned back into a multi-billion-dollar organization.

The guy is a deeply compassionate man and a wise soul who decided to analyse what the secret is to life and the key to getting results. When I read about Kazuo, we changed the entire way we work our company.

It's been said that any fool can make something more complicated, but it takes a genius to simplify it. What he figured out was that anyone who wants to have a successful life, only needs to gauge themselves on three metrics, and if they score highly in all three, their success is guaranteed.

- **Metric One: Attitude**

    Attitude is scored from negative 100 to plus 100. Since it's calculated by multiplication, if you get a negative on attitude, the rest of your score is negative.

    The reason he scored it this way is because he worked out that if you have a bad attitude, no matter what you do, you're going to bring the whole team down.

    For instance, you take a negative, low-vibrating entity and put it into a roomful of people. If those people don't have what's called energetic integrity, they can bring the energy down through entrainment, or synching with the more dominant vibration.

    When you lower your vibration, your thoughts go lower and more depressive, and when you raise your vibration, your thoughts become higher and more elated.

So if you have a bad attitude, your life is going to be miserable.

▸ Metric Two: Effort

Kazuo understood that you can't put out negative effort, so it has to be scored from zero to 100.

So, if you decide to go to the gym, but then put in minimal effort, you're not going to get the results you want.

▸ Metric Three: Ability

If you have a fantastic attitude and put in a great level of effort, the only thing that will let you down is your skill level.

For example, let's say you go to the gym and put in more effort than anyone you've ever seen, but you never ask the proper way to use the equipment, so you expend a lot of energy with little result.

Or maybe you want a better relationship, so you make sure you dedicate an hour of your day to your partner, but you spend the entire time yelling at them.

By excelling at the three elements of attitude, effort and ability, anything can happen, because all of them combined equals myelination.

Be responsible for your life. Have a positive attitude, put in the effort and acquire the right skills.

If you want to fix your finances, have a good attitude about money. Stop saying you hate it and it's not important. Then put in the effort, such as doing something every week that will improve your financial outlook.

If you do all of this, in a short period of time, you'll change your situation. There's no trick to it, but there are ways to develop these abilities, skills, efforts and attitudes, far more rapidly.

Reading doesn't change your life. Applying what you read does. There are people who are into what's called *shelf help* and *shelf development*. It's where you stand back and marvel over your shelf full of manuals.

But what you need to be concerned about is self-development, which means opening up the manual again and acting on it. Because if you're not taking any action, nothing is going to occur. The key to success is the application of knowledge.

A lot of people are reading books, thinking they're going to change, but they don't make the time to do the wonderful techniques contained in these books, because they're too busy running to read the next one.

People don't rise to the level of their expectations; they fall to the level of their training. How is it that after a year of having the exact same teacher, do certain students shine, while others don't?

It has to do with whether you have a short or long-term vision.

When you take someone who practices a musical instrument just twenty minutes a day but has a long-term vision, and compare them to someone who practices ninety minutes a day and has a short-term vision, the person who practices just twenty minutes will reach their goal five times faster. And here's something else to think about. If you get two people who practice the same ninety minutes, but one has a short-term vision and one a long term, the person with the long-term vision has a four-hundred percent greater success rate.

Inside every person is an identity; an idea of who they want to become. Maybe it's expressed or maybe it isn't, but that identity, once activated, allows them to achieve goals five times faster than anybody else. This means if it takes a person five years to write a book, you could do it in one.

This is because the myelin wrapping is accelerated when that myelin is directly correlated to your future identity. So when you line up your goals to your values, which are nothing more than the identity of who you want to be, you start to create remarkable changes.

If a child believes they're going to be a pianist for the rest of their life, as in, their identity is, "I am a pianist," when they go to rehearsal, they practice like a pianist. But somebody who says, "I'm playing the piano until the end of the year" will practice just enough to learn what they have to.

The level of attention to the activity is dramatically enhanced when your identity is true to your activity. This is why I say to people, "If you're not doing what you love, whatever you're doing is a total waste of your life."

This is because if you're doing what you love, you're going to get there five times faster, but if you're not, you'll constantly be miserable, because everyone is outperforming you and succeeding way quicker than you are. By doing what you love, you activate all of the success resources of a long-term vision.

Now, I know many people have learned to make "I am" statements, but I'm going to say something that tends to make people angry: it's a waste of time. If you want your identity statements to work, you have to change it to, *I am, because ... (of this action)*. For example, you'd say, "I am an author, because I write books."

It was discovered that the identity statement, when backed up with action, equalled results. Just saying, "I am happy" isn't enough. You have to say, "I am happy, because I hang out at the beach." Otherwise, your brain doesn't know why you're happy.

What does this mean for you? It means you need to start aligning with your vision and live true to your values. Start doing what you love. Stop following anybody else's vision, because if you do you're going to be five times slower than they are, and every day will be disappointing and leave you wondering, *Why haven't I made it yet?* The answer is, because it's not your vision. And if it's not your vision, you won't produce myelin the same way.

How does a person's values relate to their identity?

Your values play a big part in the formation of your identity. In fact, if you speak to people who study psychology, healing or transformative tools of any description, they'll explain that your identity is made up fundamentally of two things: your values, as in what you deem to be important to you, and your beliefs, as in what you believe to be true at any given moment. There are more aspects, like your capabilities, the environment you live in and your behaviours, but essentially who you are as a person consists of your values and beliefs.

When you talk to somebody and try to gauge their identity, what you're really figuring out is their values and beliefs. The stronger your identity, the faster you develop that myelin.

Your whole world is shaped by your values, so when you look at the world, you're filtering predominantly through your value systems. In other words, if your profession is collecting garbage, all you'll see are rubbish bins and how to angle your truck to pick them up. Or if you're a property developer, all you'll see are property opportunities.

To put it in more practical terms, I'd like to discuss joint bank accounts and why I disagree with them.

If a couple both pulls from the same pool of money, and it's only spent in accordance with one person's values, the by-product is called resentment, which then builds up, and all of a sudden you have a breakdown in the relationship. Forty percent of all divorces have to do with disagreements over money.

One person is going to have this thing in the back of their head, just ticking away, which leads to arguments and divorce, all because they couldn't have an open conversation about how to spend the money.

How can people resolve value conflicts and move forward?

Value conflicts can be both internal and external, meaning you can get into arguments with yourself.

Once you know your values, you can start to engineer your life to fulfil them. There are two ways to be successful in life:

1. Change your values to match your goals. (Not recommended)

2. Set your goals to match your values. (Recommended)

Most people set their goals to match other people's values, and they wonder why life is so hard. What I say to them is, "You've got to get on track and then have a crack." What I mean is that you have to get onto your values track, and then have a go. Don't have a go at life if you're not living true to your values.

There's a process to run through that will allow you to get clear about what your values are. It's called the values track, in which you identify five core categories that are important to you. Once you identify them, you can start to have a look at your identity.

But first, you need to get the base-level values sorted out and move on from there. If you don't get on track before having a crack at life, you're wasting your time. These are the five core categories:

1. **Talk**

    There are certain subjects you love talking about and ones you hate talking about.

When people talk outside of your values, you don't like them, and when they talk inside of your values, you love them. Given the opportunity, you will direct the conversation to something you enjoy talking about. You can't stop it.

2. **Research**

Would you admit that when no one else is around, you do research? You just get online or open up books. You can research until 3:00 in the morning, and not one person asked you to do it.

3. **Improve skills and abilities**

You might practice the guitar or singing or writing. There are abilities you get better at, and the reason is because you value and love them.

4. **Daydream**

There are some things you contemplate more than others. You have to get in touch with what those are and how they make you feel. For instance, you may daydream about travelling, and the feeling you get from it is freedom.

5. **Knowledge**

Inside your mind, you have bucketloads of knowledge. Some of it is completely disorganised, and some of it is really, really organised. If your knowledge is organised, this is a direct indicator that you love it, because you only organise what you love, and you disorganise what you don't.

For example, you may know how to knit, but it's not one of your favourite activities, so each step of the process may come slowly to you, whereas you love making lasagne and do it all the time, so you could quickly rifle off the steps to make it.

Disorganising a relationship is a symptom that you're falling out of love with the person. If you stop organising time and quality conversations together, it's the first indicator that you're falling out of love with them. You disorganise things to move away from them, and you organise what you enjoy.

Inside your mind you have information that's organised and you're proficient at. Whether you admit it or not, it's in there.

So, let's say your values track included healing, spirituality, presenting and travel, but you make a living as an accountant. This means you're off-track. Or even if you own your own business, but it has nothing to do with those values, you're still off-track.

Now if you travel the world speaking about spirituality and healing, you're totally on track.

So the fact is, you may know your values track, but you don't always give yourself permission to live true to it. Just because you know your values, doesn't mean you live them. There are people out there who say your life demonstrates your values, but it's not really true. Your life demonstrates your beliefs until you remove them, and then it demonstrates your values. You could be trapped by your own belief systems.

How does a person's belief system play into their value system?

If every time you try to escape you hit a wall, it means you're stuck in your belief systems. Psychologists call this your boundary conditions.

So if you know your values are spirituality, healing, presenting and travel, but you're an accountant, and someone asks why you don't travel the world sharing spiritual knowledge, your response might be, "Because I'm not smart enough" or, "It won't pay the bills" or maybe, "Well, because my dad was an accountant, and my mum was an accountant, and her mum was an accountant." These are all beliefs.

So your values are trapped inside of your belief systems, and until you shift your beliefs, you'll never live a life true to your values. But the good news is that you can destroy these beliefs, and once you clear them out, your values are then free to express themselves throughout your life.

There are those who refuse to live true to their values track. They say, "Oh, this thing? It won't pay the bills, so I'll just keep doing what I hate." But there are people out there who do what they love, and they still have bills. So if you're never going to be able to get rid of your bills, you may as well just go for it.

My advice is to do your best to get fully on track, but this is hard to do when the beliefs are blocking you, so seek knowledge as to what your values might be.

How does someone achieve a long-term vision?

Let's say you get through all of your filters: Fear, doubt, danger, suspicion, complication, boredom and uncertainty. At this point you have eight specific functions that when you turn them all on, will create miraculous goal achievement. If you see people who just accomplish things as if by magic, and you can't work out how the heck they did it, it's because these eight specific functions in their brain all switched on at once.

To reinforce the concept, I'd like to give you an example of how powerful it is when you're able to accomplish this, which is rare and only happens when you have a good reason for doing it. If you don't, you may only switch on two or three, but rarely all eight. By linking them all together with the highest density of myelin, you'll become a fully functioning human being who can achieve anything.

For instance, let's say I asked you to come up with $15,000 in five hours. You'd probably say it was impossible.

But what if I kidnapped the person you loved most in the world. Would your answer change? This example is used all the time in personal development, but few people ever bother to explain the process to you, so I'd like to do that.

When you had no reason to acquire the money, you didn't turn on the eight essential functions that are required to manifest it out of thin air.

The question is, why did the situation have to get to such extremes before you started to get resourceful? Because something did change in your psychology. Something clicked. And it was these eight functions.

So someone kidnaps a person you love, and all of a sudden you find the money. How did you go from having nothing to having $15,000 on the spot? The answer is that you started becoming resourceful, because you had to stretch your mind to think of every possibility.

Jim Rohn has a famous quote that Tony Robbins picked up and made even more famous: "It's never a matter of resources. It's only a matter of resourcefulness."

The $15,000 was always waiting for you out there, you just needed to be resourceful in the way you acquired it. That resourcefulness can only occur when eight functions in your brain start working. And when they do, you become infinitely resourceful, because you have a strong Why. Straight away you're borrowing money...you're selling your car... you're busking...you're taking a loan.

So here's a situation where you believe you can't afford to pay your rent or go on holidays, but yet if the situation called for it, you'd be able to come up with $15,000 in five hours. This is proof that you're not going to make money in any of your ventures, until you have a strong Why. Your wealth is waiting for you to find it.

This series of eight functions working together is known as the executive function.

Once this happens, you can manifest what you want out of thin air. Though I used the money example, because it's clean and quick, it could be anything, such as emotions, health and relationships. The executive function's job, if you listen carefully, is instantaneous goal achievement.

When you turn on executive function, it goes beyond myelin production and to a whole other threshold of achievement. Each individual component has different functions, but when you get all eight working together and ask, "What is the core function of those eight functions?" the answer is the achievement of goals. That is its sole job description. Not the setting of goals. Not the visualising of goals. Not the strategising of goals. The actual achievement of the goal itself. The completion of the task.

Here are the eight factors that make up executive function:

1. **Impulse control**

   The first thing that happens when you have a meaningful Why is that you immediately get impulse control. This is when you're doing a task, but you get an impulse to maybe check your social media, eat a piece of chocolate cake or stare at the television, but instead of riding the impulse, you choose to stay on task.

   If you don't have a strong Why, then when a strong impulse comes up, instead of controlling it, you act upon it and therefore don't get to where you were headed.

   So, impulse control is the ability to stop and think before acting, which happens when you possess a meaningful Why and have activated executive function.

2. **Organisation**

    When you activate executive function, organisation kicks in. This is the ability to create and maintain systems and keep track of information materials and resources to achieve your goal.

3. **Self-monitoring**

    Self-monitoring is when you're aware of who you are and monitor and evaluate your own performance. Functions of what's classed as the third eye, such as having awareness, doing meditations, scanning yourself and observing who you are as a person, are an executive function. Spiritually, it's called, awareness. So when you have awareness of the self, the body, soul or emotions, it means you've strengthened the executive function of self-monitoring.

4. **Emotional control**

    Emotional control is when you say, "I can manage my feelings by thinking appropriately about my goals." If you can't control your emotions, it has a huge impact on your achievement of goals.

    In fact, Warren Buffet said that if you can't manage your emotions, you shouldn't ever expect to manage your money. So, your emotions have a huge impact on your ability to achieve a goal, but if you keep getting swayed emotionally from side to side, you'll never follow through with it. Many people lose their goal achievement because of their emotional state. One little snafu happens, and they snap. They get annoyed for five weeks, finally get over it, and then another little thing happens, and they snap. Two years later, nothing has changed, because their executive function is broken.

5. **Flexibility**

    If you have flexibility, it means when things don't go your way, you just bend, and move, and flex around the whole idea. You have the ability to change strategies and revise plans when conditions change.

Those who are inflexible are locked into one pathway, and any deviation affects their emotions. They get angry and annoyed. These people can suspend or halt a team project, due to their refusal to bend.

6. **Working memory**

Working memory is the ability to kick up a memory into your conscious mind and use it to get the task to happen faster. When you go to take off your watch, you bring up the memory of previous times you've taken it off, hold it in your working memory, and follow it.

If you couldn't access your working memory, everything would slow down. You'd have to start all over again from the beginning, like you'd never done it before, so working memory has to be functioning in order for you to rapidly achieve your goals.

7. **Task initiation**

Task initiation is having the ability to recognise when it's time to get started on a task without delay. Procrastination is the symptom of an ineffective Why. If you don't have a good reason for doing an activity, the executive function of task initiation won't start. And if task initiation isn't working, all you experience is procrastination. So, it's the symptom of a weakness in your task initiation function.

If you decide on doing a task but put it off until you've had your coffee, or it can only be done at a certain time, and that time keeps getting pushed up until you keep promising yourself you'll complete it 'tomorrow', it's because of an ineffective executive function.

8. **Planning and prioritisation**

   Planning and prioritisation is the ability to create steps to reach a goal and make decisions as to what to focus on. It's where the brain actively shifts through the highest priorities and recalibrates itself based on the very next thing that needs to happen.

   Now, if you're able to turn on your executive function during an emergency, such as someone kidnapping your loved one and having to find a way to come up with the money, it means you already have it. But if you can't find the money the first time around, it's evidence you're not using your executive function, because in a life-or-death situation, it should become activated.

   When executive function is working correctly, you can't be distracted by anything. If someone were to come to you and ask you to goof off on social media, play a video game or watch TV, you wouldn't even answer them, because you'd be so focused on accomplishing your goal. Once executive function turns on, you can't be distracted or affected emotionally.

   Imagine you're trying to acquire the $15,000, and someone came up to you and said, "You're a loser." Do you honestly think you're going to get upset by that? No way. You don't have time. You're on project. You're on task.

   People who live true to their *Why* are not emotional, because they don't have time to react to other people's opinions. They're too busy completing an important task. Once executive function is switched on, impulses go, tasks get initiated and distractions vanish, because they're on task. That's the power of turning on executive function.

   So if you're wondering what's best to myelinate, it's all eight of these functions. There are scientists who say that it breaches back into other different parts of the lobes around your head, but most of it is found in the white and grey matter of the prefrontal region.

Do you believe science and spirituality are intertwined?

The brain is lazy by default. It follows something called the *Tao Te Ching*, which is the path of least resistance, in order to conserve energy.

Today, science and spirituality are getting closer than ever before. I think there are many concepts in spirituality that science hasn't caught up with yet, and who knows if they ever will, but the overlap between the two ideas can now be understood.

In fact, you don't even have to believe in spirituality anymore, because there's so much science that can back up anything that spiritual people say. I like to have a holistic balance. I come from a deeply spiritual background, but I also believe in the science.

For instance, if someone is clairvoyant (clear seeing), it means their imagination conjures up pictures. Being clairaudient (clear hearing) means being able to hear their imagination and pay attention to their mind chatter. Being clairsentient (clear sensing) means picking up on energies, such as walking into a building or meeting someone and instantly feeling comfortable or awkward in their presence. Having claircognizance (clear knowing) is just "knowing" something. For instance, overhearing someone talk about a certain class on a subject and feeling compelled to ask about it. Or maybe feeling the need to rush home due to sensing a loved one is in danger.

But whether you come from the four clairs or from the science, it doesn't really matter. They're all talking about the same thing. Scientists would say you're turning on executive function to the highest level. Mystics would say if you awaken the soul and the third eye, the universe will writhe at your feet in ecstasy as it conspires for your greatness.

What they're talking about is the capacity to master manifest. But no matter which theory you believe, it's the ability to create miracles in your life. It truly is.

So if you can wire the eight executive functions together and consciously strengthen them, you'll become a goal-achieving machine. Anything you want to create in life is yours for the taking, because to try and achieve a goal without one of them would be a challenging experience.

Unless you had a major traumatic head injury, then chances are your executive function is going for it. And even if you did experience trauma, the good news is that you can just myelinate it starting today. You can rewire all of this stuff and wrap it with no problem at all.

I want you to understand this, because once you do, you'll realise you can accomplish anything and change your life.

 To discover more about how Ben can help you *Elevate Your Mindset*, simply visit www.elevatebooks.com/mindset

Patty Duque

Harness Your Happiness

Patty Duque is an internationally certified Coach, speaker and author, who's made it her mission to help people harness their true and unique joy.

Patty believes happiness isn't derived from a 'to-do' or 'to-have' list but from an inner knowledge, awareness, understanding and strength that comes from striving for it every day. Her satisfaction comes from helping people improve their mindset, relationships, health, career and finance, including those who believe they're living a comfortable life and are unaware of how much better it could be if they harnessed their happiness.

Patty's travels and life experiences have taught her to be authentic and search within for her own happiness.

Patty Duque

Harness Your Happiness

What's your biggest life lesson?

My biggest life lesson is that happiness comes from within. You don't need to look for happiness in others, and definitely not in external or material things that only bring momentary joy.

Take the time to learn about yourself. Become aware of your emotions, actions, reactions, likes, dislikes, and more importantly, the meaning you give to life. The better in tune, accepting and comfortable you are with yourself, the clearer your meaning will be and the happier you will feel.

Changing your perception and the meaning of your story will free you from long-term pain and help you to stop feeling helpless and unworthy.

Everyone has a choice to be a victim or remain in a state of acceptance and joy. Be yourself and consciously choose to live a happy and fulfilled life. This means acknowledging past circumstances but not allowing them to define you. Instead, learn from them, accept that the past can't be changed and focus on the future and moving on.

Most people have expectations as to how life should be and base their happiness on whether or not circumstances go their way. But that isn't true happiness.

If you're more aware of yourself, your emotions and your triggers, you won't let these moments define you for years to come. You alone have the power to change your perception and reaction.

Every choice you make based on your inner-voice and the stories it tells you, influences how you live your life. The quicker you learn this, the less you'll suffer.

> "The quality of your life depends on the quality of your thoughts." ~ Marcus Aurelius

Your perceptions have an effect on your day-to-day life and wellbeing.

Having positive thoughts will attract positive energy and positive people, and good things will happen as a result. It has nothing to do with luck.

What was the most difficult time in your life, and how did you overcome it?

At the age of nine, my life was turned upside down when family moved to Japan.

I was born in Colombia, South America and lived there most of my childhood years. I only spoke Spanish, and all of a sudden my schooling was in English, while my 'street life' was in Japanese. I felt completely lost and out of my comfort zone, attending a school with so many different nationalities, and every day I'd have to navigate one of the most complex train systems in the world.

The first year was tough, to say the least. In Colombia, I'd been attending a co-ed school. In Japan, my parents placed me in an all-girls Catholic school. Though it was run by nuns who spoke Spanish in case I needed any support, for the first three months while I learnt English, I was basically mute and therefore had difficulty making friends. Anyone who knows me would think this to be almost impossible, but I now recognise it taught me how to acclimate in different and challenging environments.

I was vulnerable, and being unable to communicate resulted in getting bullied. I hated going to school and being in Japan, and I just wanted to go back to my comfort zone in Bogota. For a social butterfly like I am, having only a couple of friends that weren't even in my grade level was incredibly hard!

I have the most loving and supportive family. The move was a hard adjustment for everyone in our own ways, but my parents did what they thought was best for us. They worked hard to provide the finest education and amazing opportunities few kids my age would have experienced. By the age of fourteen, I'd visited just under twenty countries, which opened my eyes to different cultures, religions and languages. I became a 'citizen of the world'.

My parents taught us to be authentic and have roots, while at the same time giving us wings to fly as high as we wanted. But I couldn't grasp that concept at the time and only understood I felt alone and different.

Being the youngest of the family, I was spoiled and was looked after by my older brother and sister. In Colombia, it was my brother's responsibility to pick me up when I'd attend parties as a condition of letting me go in the first place. He'd help me with my homework and educate me about life.

My sister was my buddy and always protected me. We laughed and tried to make the best of our years in Japan, as for both of us it was such a surreal situation, like being in a movie. It strengthened our bond.

However, for some reason my brother, who's six years my senior, thought it would be funny to tell everyone I was adopted. Maybe he thought it was a harmless prank, or it was his way of dealing with the change, and wasn't aware of how this would impact me. But the effect was that not only did I feel isolated at school, I saw myself as totally different from the very people I should have felt closest to: my family.

As a child, all I wanted was to fit in and be accepted. Yet despite the school's diversity, I still managed to stand out and get picked on.

I even thought of taking my own life and would plan how I could jump off the balcony just outside my bedroom, which was located on the second floor. Of course, I would have landed in a beautiful bed of flowers, so the maximum damage might have been a broken bone, but the thought was certainly there. I cried myself to sleep almost every night for ten consecutive months.

But once I realised this was only causing me emotional pain, I decided to change my way of thinking and hit the reset button. I became 'me' again and started seeing my situation in a much more positive light. Now, thirty years later, I have the fondest memories and lifelong friendships from my time in Japan.

Though I didn't know it at the time, this single event changed the direction of my life and made me no longer want to be a victim but to habitually alter my perception of challenging situations and see an optimal solution.

> "Happiness is a choice, not a result!
> Nothing will make you happy until you choose to be happy.
> No person will make you happy unless you decide to be happy.
> Your happiness will not come to you; it can only come from you!"
> ~ Ralph Marston

What do you think is your life purpose?

I'd never thought about this until I attended an event where I was asked this exact question. While others around me struggled to answer, it was so clear in my mind that at first I thought I'd gotten it wrong. But once I said it out loud, I knew it was right.

I believe my purpose in life is to shine and harness happiness in myself and those around me.

I know I'm here to contribute and serve others. I've always done it in one way or another, so when I realised this was my purpose, building my business around it was a no-brainer.

How would you like to be remembered?

I would love to be remembered as someone who was brave and lived life to the fullest, raised her standards, seized all opportunities, and regardless of what came her way, always looked on the bright side of life.

How do you start your day?

I'm an early riser. When I first get up, I meditate for ten to fifteen minutes and say some affirmations. Also, to get my endorphins going, I do an intense workout, a blissful yoga class or a challenging boxing session. This helps me stay mentally fit and excited about my day.

How do you finish your day?

I lead such a busy life that it's easy to forget to be grateful. Therefore, as part of our nightly routine before we go to bed, my family and I share three things we're grateful for.

Taking the time to reflect upon what I'm thankful for brings me happiness and makes me feel more alive.

What do you think the biggest issues are that block people from finding happiness?

I think people confuse happiness with having fun. This is far from the truth, as fun comes from external influences, while happiness comes from within.

Happiness is about being in the moment. It's having contentment with where you are, who you've become, and above all, feeling at peace within yourself. Fun, on the other hand, is what you do to enjoy yourself momentarily and at times distract yourself from unhappy thoughts.

By understanding this fundamental difference, the cloud will lift, and you will accept yourself and your circumstances, as well as gain clarity as to what's holding you back.

I've been living in Australia since 2000, and when I go back to Colombia for a visit, friends often ask, "How can you be happy living so far away from your home and your loved ones?" As I truly believe happiness comes from within, I struggle with these types of comments. In this day and age, when technology allows you to communicate whenever you want from anywhere in the world, distance shouldn't be an obstacle to doing what makes you happy and following your dreams.

How can people be happier in life?

These are what I consider the thirteen secrets to harnessing your happiness:

1. **Remember that attitude is everything**

    Choose to be happy. Changing your thoughts will impact everything around you. Make this a habit.

2. **Be open to change**

   Happiness isn't a product of one thing but the sum of many. Embrace this new lifestyle.

3. **Look after yourself**

   Your mind, body and soul combined are the vehicle to happiness.

4. **Take time out**

   Take time for yourself, and try to quiet down your conscious mind, so your subconscious can be heard.

5. **Be yourself, be brave and be proud of it**

   Look within yourself, and your strengths will flourish.

6. **Differentiate between dreams and goals**

   If you put a due date on a dream, you'll convert it into an achievable goal.

7. **Forgive and forget**

   Take a minute to forgive, and avoid a life sentence of resentment. Don't be your own prisoner.

8. **Remind yourself that the secret of living is giving**

   Go out of your way to help someone or give them an unexpected gift. The universe will pay you back two-fold when you least expect it.

9. **Recognise that you're the sum of the people you surround yourself with**

   Positive people will always bring sunshine to your life.

10. **Acknowledge that clarity is power**

    Understand what drives you, fulfils you and what really, really matters to you.

11. **Be thankful**

    The spiritual experience of living every minute with gratitude will fill your soul.

12. **Smile often**

    Smiling relaxes the muscles and costs less than electricity but provides more light.

13. **Maintain a balancing act**

    To attain happiness and reap the benefits of achieving your goal, incorporate your changes into your everyday life.

Do you have an approach to happiness?

My HAPPY 5-step framework helps you harness your happiness, which means defining what ultimately makes YOU happy, takes you to a place of contentment and brings success and fulfilment into your life. Below is a diagram that outlines each step.

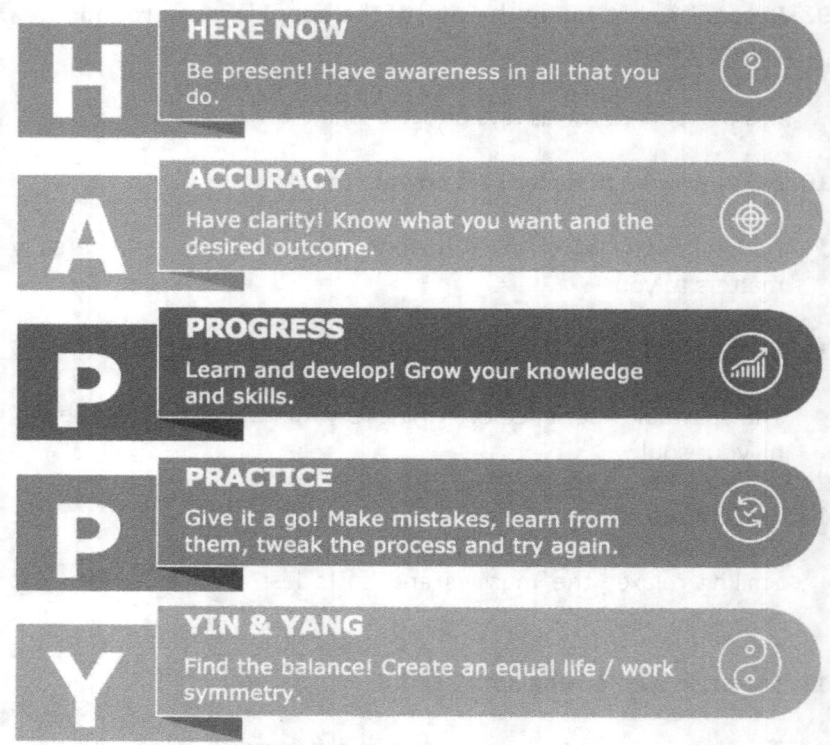

Here Now

It's important to start by acknowledging where you are. Be present. Take a minute to stay still, embrace your surroundings, use your senses and take it all in.

Accuracy

Be specific as to what you really want and the outcomes you'd like to achieve.

<u>P</u>rogress

In order to get ahead, it's important to grow, so learn and develop your skills. Do your research: read, listen to leaders in the area you want to master, go to seminars and take courses. Become hungry for knowledge. Accept disparate views and decide where you stand. Don't be afraid to be different.

<u>P</u>ractice

Give it a go! Everyone needs to start somewhere, so practice, practice, practice, and be authentic in new ways.

<u>Y</u>in and Yang

The ancient symbol of harmony depicts life as a balancing act that's most fulfilling when you learn to embrace its dualities, the good and the bad. Once you learn to harness your own happiness, you'll be more able to balance your work and home life. Make appointments with yourself and stick to them. It will help you connect with yourself and transform. You, and everyone around you, will benefit from it.

> "Happiness is when what you think,
> what you say and what you do are in harmony"
> ~Mahatma Gandhi

How did you get started with your business, and what did you have to overcome to build it?

I was happy in my job as a managing consultant, but as time passed I felt something was missing. I'd been in the corporate world for sixteen years, in the consulting industry for over twelve and the same organisation for almost eight, but I was only operating at my full potential when connecting with my colleagues and clients as individuals.

During working hours, I would always make time for people who reached out to me needing support or to open up to someone. I created great friendships, and instead of prioritising my work, I would prioritise their needs. I'd spend time talking to them and understanding their situation. I valued building rapport and trust and would stay up late or wake up early to get my work done, whether it was for my clients, my work colleagues or my friends. It was rewarding to help people grow, but I never thought something that came so naturally, and I enjoyed so much, could be my job.

Then I started listening to a faint voice that had been getting louder and louder. I knew I wanted to do something that was purpose-driven and aligned with my passion for helping others but didn't see how I could make the transition. Then my instinct drew me to a coach who helped me realise I'd been mentoring and empowering people in many ways for most of my adult life.

After becoming a mother of two, I had less and less time, so when the idea of becoming a coach came up, it felt right. However, I struggled and felt uncomfortable with the idea of asking people to pay for what I considered to be 'friendship'. I undervalued my ability, until my coach made me realise that while yes, I was being a friend, I was also adding value by challenging them and changing their lives more than any of their other friends could.

I had to overcome my belief that I couldn't charge for my services. People tend to invest in momentary happiness, but not in anything long-term, until tragedy strikes. They're often scared to go deeper. They don't want to face their fears, their past, their limiting beliefs or even find their purpose. They tend to think it's all too hard. They silence their doubts by telling themselves that everything is okay, but deep inside they ignore their inner voice and wonder why others can do it and they can't. For fear of asking for help, or not knowing what to ask for, they choose inaction.

If you're not where you want to be, then clearly what you're doing isn't getting results. In order to progress, you need to change, and the quickest way to do it is by getting the right support.

As the famous quote goes, "The definition of insanity is doing the same thing over and over again, expecting different results."

People tend to think that coaches are only for successful people with big dreams, like Olympians and millionaires. But in reality, they accomplished these remarkable results because they had coaches.

My coach showed me how to value the benefits of having a sounding board that isn't part of my family, circle of friends or work environment. Most people long to have someone they can reach out to, who can provide a space where they can be honest, talk openly about their struggles without shame or guilt, and most importantly, get held accountable for their results.

After acquiring my first paying client and achieving great results, I started valuing my work more and more. I realised that when there's an exchange of money, the level of commitment alters the dynamic, as the client now has skin in the game and understands it's up to them to get the results they want. I can only guide and keep them accountable. I can't do the work for them.

What's the biggest tip you could give a client?

By obtaining clarity as to what you want, you will be able to master your mindset. The inner chatter kills dreams, paralyses you and can make you procrastinate or give up. This is why you can feel like years have passed, and you're still stuck on a hamster wheel.

Getting clarity, staying focused and knowing your purpose, will give meaning to your life and awaken the desire to grow and develop, which ultimately leads to living a purposeful, happy life.

What's the best way people can achieve a good life-work balance?

I think the best way is by scheduling activities that make you happy and commit to doing them. Like everything else in life, you need to make time for what matters most, feeds your soul, allows you to grow and gives you fulfilment. Don't let work take precedence and overrule the time set aside to do what you love.

People are more productive when they have breaks, as it allows the energy to flow around their body. This can be done by going for a walk, calling a friend, listening to music, reading or listening to a TED Talk. Scheduling the activity in a diary gives it importance. No matter what happens, make sure not to cancel it or leave it for 'tomorrow' or 'another time'.

Think of it like a bank account you need to keep topping up, or else you're left with nothing. At times when life gets so busy, you forget to stop and think about your emotional balance and only notice something's wrong when you become rundown, which is usually a good signal from your body that you need to take a break.

You know you've nailed it when the behaviour becomes a habit, and you no longer need to schedule it.

Why is mindset important?

The name says it all. Master your mind, and success will follow.

Your body won't move until your mind tells it to, so unless you start empowering your mind with positive thoughts, you won't get amazing results. As with every other muscle in your body, get into the habit of training your mind in order to achieve the outcomes you want.

> "My inner world creates my outer world"
> ~T. Harv Eker

What importance does mindset play in setting goals?

You can have the best plan in the world, but if your mind isn't convinced, you won't achieve it.

Last year I was asked to do a talk about mindset, and I narrowed it down to three key words people use daily, so they'd be easy to remember and would give them the opportunity to question themselves. These are:

1. **Why?**

   ▶ *Why do I want to achieve this, and why is it important to me?*

   I believe that without clarity, you're bound to fail in achieving your goal. You may get instant results, but they won't be long-term. Whatever you want to achieve in whatever area of your life, ask yourself, *Why do I want _____ (fill in the blank)?*

   You can do this by continuing to ask yourself that same question at least five times, going deeper and deeper each time. Keep asking it, until you hit an emotion. The stronger the emotion, the more defining it will be. That's when you know you have a strong WHY. *Dig deep, and it will stick!*

   Example: *Why do I want to lose weight?*

   - Because I want to fit into my favourite jeans.

   - Because when I used to wear those jeans, I felt confident and got so many compliments.

- Because I had endless energy and felt I could do anything.

- Because I could run around after my kids and enjoy life with them.

- Because my parents didn't have the health or fitness to create these types of memories with me and my siblings, so I want my kids to remember me as someone who was able to participate in their lives.

You can see that by going deep, it was revealed that the goal of losing weight had nothing to do with fitting into jeans but instead with the ability to break a cycle that brought so much sadness and provided enough fire in the belly to succeed.

2. What?

▶ *What outcome would I like to achieve?*

Unless you set a goal, measure it, have a long-term vision and create an identity, it's difficult to reach the desired outcome. You can't improve what you don't measure. Start by setting clear goals that will support the identity of who you want to become.

There are many ways to set goals. Just pick one that works for you, and ensure the steps take you outside your comfort zone, as this is where the real magic happens. If you're clear on what your top three values are, you'll be able to set and align your goals with them and not go astray. For example, if having vitality and optimal health is one of your highest values, but you live a lifestyle that contradicts it and instead are a couch potato or party animal, you'll feel out of alignment and waste so much energy undoing all of your unsupportive actions.

This is the reason people will binge one day then wake up feeling so horrible, all they want to do is some physical exercise.

After setting a concise goal, create an identity. Have an exact picture in your head and talk to yourself as if you've already achieved it. Think about how you would dress, act and speak, the people you'd socialise with and places you'd go. For example, instead of thinking, *I want to fit into my size twelve jeans,* you'll instead switch your focus to, *I'm now a size twelve*, and then everything you'd do once you accomplish it. Make sure your vision is long-term.

3. How?

▸ *How can I achieve this?*

There are plenty of strategies to achieving your goals. Find the one that works for you, and stick to it. I'll use the example of someone who wants to save money, as this and being healthy are two of the most common goals.

❖ **Stay present and focused**

- Don't think of the end goal of saving $10,000. Just start by focusing on small amounts first. Every time you're about to spend money, ask yourself, *Do I really need this?*

❖ **Get visual**

- Create a vision board or put up pictures that represents your goal where you can see them every day.

❖ **Create a habit**

- Start a habit that supports your goal, like limiting the number of times you buy lunch or coffees on your work days. You'll be surprised how much this equates to in a year.

❖ **Schedule it**

- Every month, schedule a set amount of your pay that goes into a savings account. Make the time to record your transactions, so you have a clear understanding of where your money is going.

❖ **Find a balance**

- Make sure it's not all about saving. Leave yourself with some money for spending freely. If needed, have two different accounts, one for spending and the other for saving.

❖ **Accountability**

- Get an accountability partner who calls you out when you're not sticking to your goal.

If you're able to nail the why, what and how, there will be no stopping you from harnessing your happiness.

What's one of the biggest goals you've achieved?

Apart from building my own business, I would say getting my Australian residency. For some, it may sound like an easy and straightforward process, but believe me, I had to jump through some unbelievable hoops.

You see, I originally came to Australia because it was my best friend's dream to live there. When I was in Montreal, she visited me and planted the seed of going to Australia together to study for our last year of university. I'd deferred my degree for a semester to go to Canada, so I still had to complete my thesis in order to finalise it. We'd always wanted to live overseas together, so without any hesitation we both applied, got accepted, and before we knew it, were in Sydney studying for our honours.

I never had the intention of staying permanently, given the distance from home, but within the first year, Australia grew on me. I fell in love with the lifestyle, the culture and the people. I felt so at home.

After finishing our studies, my best friend headed back to Colombia, while I went to Brisbane, as I wasn't ready to part with this amazing country. I was open to anything that would give me the opportunity to stay longer, so I managed to get a job in the mining industry. I ended up moving to Townsville and later to Wollongong, which meant starting over each time I arrived in a new city.

I eventually ended up back in Brisbane, where I live now. The more I explored, the more at home I felt. And when I decided to apply for my residency, my only thought was, *How hard could it be?*

I got the answer to that question the hard way.

I applied on my own, as I didn't have the funds to go through an agency or a lawyer.

After my application sat in an overseas Australian commission for two years being processed, I was told I was five points short. The only options I had for obtaining those points was demonstrating I was bilingual, determined by a translator's exam, or investing $100,000 on a government bond, which was almost double my annual income.

I thought proving I was bilingual would be the easy option. After all, I was fluent in two languages. Well, I failed the exam! What I learned was that just because you speak another language, doesn't mean you're a translator. So, the only option left was somehow getting the money for the bond.

I tried everything, including speaking to all the major banks, but the amount was too much for a personal loan, and I needed to be an Australian to apply. This is irony at its best.

Patty Duque

I couldn't waste time, as I was given three months to get the bond, and every night I would go to bed with the image of a clock going *tick, tick, tick* and then exploding.

My mission was to get that money, as I saw it as something attainable. Just because I didn't have it, didn't mean I couldn't get it.

I had the option of borrowing part of the money from my family overseas but was concerned about the exchange rate. Currencies fluctuate, so I wanted to borrow the money in Australian dollars. Also, I desired to achieve this on my own.

After talking to everyone and seeking every opportunity I could think of, one day a couple that had basically adopted me as a daughter while I was living in Townsville, offered to help.

I couldn't even fathom the idea of borrowing that amount of money, but we signed a contract and agreed this would be treated as a business transaction. I was able to invest in the government bond as per the visa requirement, and a year later when I got the money back, I transferred it with the agreed interest rate to my silent angels.

Against all odds, and after a fair amount of failure, I was able to achieve the goal I so passionately wanted.

The irony is that at the time, I was dating my current husband, and even my boss said I should save myself the hassle, marry my boyfriend and be granted residency that way. But for me, marriage was about love and not money, so that wasn't an option. It would have saved me a lot of sleepless nights, but I couldn't do it.

When I tell this story, people often say, "I can't believe it. You're so lucky!" But what they don't take into account is that I didn't just sit and wait for money to fall into my lap. I had a clear goal, I was determined, I worked hard, and no matter what, I showed up every day accepting the difficult times and failures for what they were. When one door closed, I knew another one would open, until I was led to the least-expected door, one I wasn't even knocking on.

Why is setting goals important?

Goals keep you focused, make you push your boundaries and help you progress. Without them, you stay in limbo and wake up years later realising you haven't achieved much in life. Everyone has the same twenty-four hour day. Those who succeed have clarity, set goals around what they want and prioritise them.

> "Harnessing your happiness has to begin from within."
> ~Patty Duque

 To discover more about how Patty can help you *Elevate Your Mindset*, simply visit www.elevatebooks.com/mindset

Rani Kudhal

Mind Fitness

Rani Kudhal is a life mentor with sixteen years of experience helping people in the midst of crippling anxieties and the inability to define their life purpose, to excel in their personal and professional lives.

She's worked within a multitude of global industries. Her clients have included people from all walks of life, from CEOs to those who've fallen on hard times and wound up homeless.

Rani is highly intuitive and has a patient communication style. She has a proven ability of using her creative and practical skills to help her clients turn conceptual dreams into concrete and relevant life experiences. With her guidance, they're able to achieve multiple goals, even in times of rapid changes and tight time constraints.

Rani Kudhal
Mind Fitness

Why is mindset important?

I've had several big challenges in my life, one of which happened when I was a newlywed and was diagnosed with endometriosis. The pain was so severe that I'd collapse on the floor clutching my pelvis and would occasionally faint. The combination of the strongest prescribed painkillers wouldn't even make a difference. I'd have to lie in bed for three days and nights each month with two scalding hot water bottles on my stomach, vomiting from the pain. I couldn't have imagined anything worse.

But there was. The physical pain was nothing compared to my anguish when I discovered it caused infertility. I'd always wanted to be a mother, and when I heard this news, my entire world come crashing down around my ears. I judged myself as less of a woman and a fake. I knew logically this wasn't true, but my heart told me it was. I sank into a depression and questioned everything. I'd been a fitness freak, working as a personal trainer and life coach. I also ate well and exercised regularly, while keeping a positive mindset, so I couldn't fathom it. But I did know I had to change my thinking.

I was terrified of having an operation, because I didn't want any of it to be real. The initial laparoscopy (a surgical diagnostic procedure used to examine the organs inside the abdomen) just resulted in even more terror and anxiety. The surgeon said it was the worst case of endometriosis he'd seen in his career and let me know a second surgery would be needed immediately, with another specialist surgeon present. He gently explained that he required my consent and written permission to remove any part of my pelvis he deemed necessary and commented that he didn't know how I managed the pain. I barely absorbed his words, because all I heard was that my dream was slipping away, and the life I desperately wanted was not to be. I was crushed.

The night before I went into my second laparoscopy, I wrote myself a note I've never shared with anyone before now:

Dear Rani,

I know you're scared. I love you. God is with you.

Whatever happens tomorrow, you will be alright, and things will work out in the end, I promise.

Don't ever let ANYONE tell you that you won't be a mother. You will. No one else ever gets to decide that for you, okay? Look at what you have achieved thus far in life. You have a great Shakti *inside you. Please continue to believe and have faith, and remember God is holding your hand all the way through tomorrow.*

Shakti literally means power; it's considered the creative energy of the Divine Feminine, the Great Mother.

When I awoke from my surgery, I was told that some of my pelvis had been removed.

But I didn't lose hope. For years I kept visualising myself as a mother with a healthy, happy bouncing baby, with tiny hands and feet and cute, chubby cheeks. At the same time, I practiced and solidified a powerful manifestation process that currently helps me guide people to bring their dreams into reality in small, digestible chunks.

Four years later, my daughter was born.

It was my greatest achievement in life and my happiest mindset triumph. That day, no one could keep the smile off my face! I couldn't stop staring at her. She was a miracle. Her name means 'a gift from God' and was given to me in a dream.

My biggest regret in life would have been letting my prognosis crush my spirit.

> "The subconscious will bring into reality any picture brought continually, constantly and consistently into the mind and backed with faith."
> ~Napoleon Hill, author of Think and Grow Rich

What role do you think having faith plays in people's lives?

I have a non-traditional relationship with God. My parents studied many religions and cultures and respected them all, and for this I'm deeply grateful.

You may believe in a higher power and call it Universe, Source, Spirit, Love or whatever language fits you. There's no right or wrong. I choose to call it God and believe having faith in something greater than ourselves is important, if only to provide hope.

The opposite of faith is doubt. It makes you consistently ask yourself, *"What's the point?"* to which you'll always reply, *"There is none."*

What drives you?

When I was growing up, people didn't talk about mental illness, and 'staying happy' wasn't a subject taught at school. Mental illness, depression and anxiety deeply affected people close to me, and it scared me. All I saw was that they were prescribed these little magical pills, so I didn't know that anything other than medication was a possible cure, until I went on a personal quest to find alternative treatments.

What I found was that there are endless modalities and millions of beautiful healers who can produce effective results, and I wanted to study and implement as many of them as I could. To me, there's no greater service I can provide than to help someone heal, and I'm greatly humbled to have this opportunity to ease someone's suffering, even sixteen years on.

Having been privileged to experience thousands of meaningful insights into my clients' lives over the years, I believe I have a fair grasp of what challenges and inspires people, and I want to share the benefit of my experience and teachings.

I encourage other coaches and healers to keep going and not assume that people have the basic skills and knowledge to tackle their issues.

It's important that this empowering knowledge, along with the essential skills, be made available to those who live in remote areas and don't have access to workshops and therapists or are unable to financially invest in themselves. I want to give people hope in their most desperate times. It's what motivates me to keep going. I aspire to be a great leader in the eyes of my daughter and inspire her to have high personal standards, remain faithful and be of service to others.

I believe that the normalisation of challenges is a good thing, as many people find it hard to talk about what they've been through and therefore may not seek help. But it's also important to keep attempting to overcome these challenges. For instance, if they've had an unsatisfactory experience with a particular therapist or treatment, I tell them not to resign themselves to never getting well and that there are hundreds and thousands of ways of achieving a fulfilling and wonderful life. They just need to keep going.

I'm deeply passionate about helping people empower their inner wounded child, so they regain their faith that the game of life can once again be played with gusto.

Even if I give hope to just one more person who might be thinking of giving up, I would be so grateful.

What's the difference between what people say they want and what they need?

People say they want a lot of superficial and fun things, but ultimately, they need love, connection and purpose to create a meaningful life. They don't see the world as it is, but as they are.

Some of my clients are inspired by fame, celebrity, money and beauty. Others admire those who have an enthusiasm for learning while focussed on living their passion and staying humble, especially if it appears they've achieved happiness and financial independence along this path.

What inspires you?

Those who make mistakes and apologise, even to children and subordinates, are inspiring. I believe it shows they have respect for others and a commitment to be a great leader, parent or mentor.

People I find inspiring are happy, grateful and peaceful in their current situation. They see beauty in everything and take time out for others, even if there's no reward for themselves. It's a beautiful way to keep the human connection flowing.

What do you think is the biggest issue people deal with?

When people are unhappy, they can be angry, shallow, faithless and selfish, until eventually when they become too damaged to trust others, they might even engage in destructive behaviours and compromise their personal values.

People do notice your character and can sense if you're a decent person or masquerading as someone nice while lying and cheating. I believe there's a lot of wisdom in religious teachings that state no one is without sin and telling yourself you're 'not as bad as the next guy' doesn't make you a better person. You're not fooling anyone in the long run. Get help, and please forgive yourself.

What do you think blocks people from living their best life?

Stress goes hand in hand with city living, the extent and impact of which isn't appreciated enough. In my opinion, everyone will experience anxiety, depression, abuse or even a trauma at some stage of their life, and these can manifest into blocks that stand in the way of living their best life.

I've personally experienced a variety of abuse, and even though I've been studying the mind and behaviours for twenty years, I'm not immune to intentional or unintentional harm. It's common and can happen to anyone; however, you can develop resilience and self-care practices.

Is there a stigma related to those who experience trauma and abuse?

There is no justification for abuse. No one has the right to harm another, so don't let anyone blame you for their behaviour. You can't cause anyone to hit you, cheat on you, call you bad names or bully you. Abuse directed at you is never your fault and never, ever deserved.

If you believe there's a stigma related to being abused or traumatised, you may not be aware of how common it is. Seventy percent of Americans experience some form of trauma, and of those, twenty percent develop post-traumatic stress disorder (PTSD).

Over the years, I've learnt how to respect and acknowledge trauma and anxiety in myself and others. I've also developed methods to overcome these obstacles, as it's the only way to remain on the path to achieving dreams, goals, successes and living a life of purpose.

There have been massive developments in understanding the best treatments and triggers in trauma treatment over the past thirty years, and it's a subject I continue to study. The work being done by The National Institute for the Clinical Application of Behavioural Medicine (NICABM), in the state of Connecticut in the United States, provides information regarding pioneering treatments to therapists and sufferers worldwide.

According to the Australian institute of criminology:

- Domestic violence is the single biggest health risk to women aged 15-44.

- One in six boys, and one in four girls, experience some kind of sexual abuse, and these are only the ones that are reported.

- In regard to workplace bullying, Beyond Blue in Australia published the following:

  - One in two Australians have experienced workplace bullying in their lifetime.

  - Targets of workplace bullying have higher rates of depression, anxiety and PTSD.

  - Witnesses tend to not speak up due to fear of losing their job.

  - Many people are too ashamed to tell their families they've been bullied or unfairly dismissed and frequently feel pressured to return to the workplace while still suffering from psychological and physical injuries.

There are many legitimate causes for anxiety and depression that people are afraid to speak up about because they fear being labelled as hysterical and told they're overreacting. These include:

- Bullying

    More than half of teens using social media have been witness to, or personally been a victim of, cyber-bullying. Most of this is done via cell phone, which nearly every kid has nowadays, but schoolyard bullying is also still prevalent.

    Kids are afraid to speak up for fear of being stigmatised or getting bullied even more.

- Loss

    Loss is a major trauma that affects everyone and doesn't only constitute the death of a loved one. It can also mean estrangement from your children post separation or grieving the loss of your partner and family after a breakup. Grief isn't linear, and the impact could vary according to other aspects of your life at that time. Waves of grief can come at unpredictable times, as well as those that are expected, such as anniversaries of your loss.

    The impacts of loss are vast and can be traumatic, and you may not even be consciously aware of the effects. For instance, if you lose a parent prematurely, it can affect your ability to form a close relationship, marry and have kids or sustain a long-term, balanced relationship, even if you desperately want one. You can develop a fear of losing that person, so you unconsciously sabotage close connections. When experiencing loss, and its aftermath, it's a time to go gently. Don't let anyone scold you into believing you should be over it or that it's no big deal. When you're ready, please know there's help available to you.

Once you understand that anxiety and depression can be genetic, hereditary or symptomatic of events that have happened in your life, and you don't just label yourself as anxious or depressed, you'll understand the impact it's having on the quality of your life and develop strategies to address these seemingly chronic conditions.

You'll know it's time to seek help if you're:

- having suicidal thoughts or feelings of despair that 'things won't change'

- spending sleepless nights due to worrying

- having trouble getting out of bed or sleeping too much because of depression

- suffering from physical symptoms of panic, such as sweaty hands, elevated heart rate and feeling faint

- having feelings of worthlessness or believing others when they tell you that you'll amount to nothing

- experiencing constant bullying, whether in your home, work or online, and have no support systems in place

- lowering your personal standards to the point you're always dating the 'wrong type of person'

- feeling overwhelmed and worrying excessively

- having angry outbursts

You're enough as you are, and there's a huge community of people who love and want to help you. These issues won't magic themselves away and will only exacerbate for years to come. If any of these apply to you, now is the time to take action.

How did you go from a disempowering mindset to an empowering one?

I grew up in West London and had a heavy shame and guilt-filled upbringing. My hard-working, chronically exhausted grandmother taught me traditional Indian Sikh values. I was too young at the time to understand this wasn't true Sikhism at all, and it appeared to me that my English friends were having more fun.

I developed a victim mentality and blamed others rather than taking responsibility for my lot in life, in much the same way I witnessed the adults doing. Despite this, I had my faith and a positive and grateful outlook.

While for some members of my family and community there was an expectation I would have an arranged marriage, when I was fourteen my dad came to me and said, "I want you to be emotionally, physically and financially independent of any man". This was the crossroad when I realised I could choose my own thoughts and create my own life.

He saw through my eyes the hardships endured by females in my community who were expected to put their husbands first, and how the elder women went so far to enforce the family law, they even asked the men to beat their wives into submission. I was *outta* there!

Though there are still some communities in which this behaviour persists, I'm happy to report times are changing for the better.

Later on, I learnt how to master my thoughts and enhance my choices through official courses and self-study. I chose to go to university and travel extensively. I then lived in New York and Melbourne, before finally deciding to settle in Sydney.

To put this in perspective, twenty years ago a female travelling and living abroad alone was unheard of in my community. I had to learn to navigate the unchartered terrain, stop caring about what others said about me and develop self-approval. Throughout it all, I've received unconditional love from my mum, who I need to thank for putting herself on the line for me.

My personal journey was a rollercoaster, and that's why it's important to me that others learn from my mistakes and challenges. I want them to feel love and support along the way.

I've organised the knowledge I've gained from the many tens of thousands of dollars I've spent on courses and personal development, and I teach these techniques to empower others, so they can help themselves when I'm no longer guiding them. My goal is to make these tools available to everyone who needs them.

How do you help people with their issues?

The good news is that there's help available. Mind technologies were practiced long before scientific evidence backed up the results. I use scientifically proven, practical tools that really work and can help anyone.

These are the steps I use in my program.

▸ **Step one: Create Awareness**

Understand what is happening and why. A study conducted by Ruth M. Buczynski, PhD, President and Licensed Psychologist at NICABM, found that twenty percent of the people who developed post-traumatic stress disorder (PTSD) had some common traits.

1. They *dissociated* from the experience, which caused a fragmentation of their memory. When the internal sense of coherence is affected, this alone can be a source of trauma and contribute to feelings of confusion and feeling overwhelmed.

2. They had a *poor support network* before, during and after the trauma.

   By understanding the history and relationships the person had with protective caregivers when they were a child, you'll have insight as to the kind of support they received following a traumatic experience. For example:

   - Event: teenager experiences sexual abuse

   - Family 1(Unsupportive): "It's your fault. You dress slutty"

   - Family 2 (Supportive): "Are you okay? How can we help?"

It's true that someone will only see what's going on when they believe it, especially if they never had a healthy support structure, so this concept needs to be presented gently. Pets are a great way of introducing trust and love to people who've been abused and find it hard to accept support from others.

▶ **Step two: Create Wholeness of the Mind and Body**

Creating integration between all parts of the brain is powerful and fun. According to Ruth M. Buczynski, when the brain can't integrate itself, traumatic memories have free rein to replay in the mind time and time again.

It's important to encourage trauma victims to sleep well, eat cleanly, minimise taking any stimulants and sit in stillness whenever possible. Until they can once again discern who's safe for them, let them know that it's okay to get external feedback from those they know they can trust.

My parents have been a rock-solid example of a growth mindset. They've fervently studied all people and cultures and embrace life. My dad insists on the practice of sitting and doing nothing at all for fifteen to thirty minutes a day to realign with his intuition. This is different to prayer, which is talking to the deity of your choice, while meditation is about listening.

In my practice, I use several processes to facilitate the wholeness of the mind and body.

▶ **Step three: Reinstate Control**

The world's leading expert in the treatment of trauma, Bessel van der Kolk, M.D., says, "As long as you can tolerate what's going on right now, then there is no need for any further (psychological) treatment."

People who've experienced trauma, abuse and other hardships may feel a loss of personal control. There are simple ways to help give it back:

❖ **Be mindful of what might trigger them**

Abusers often win the trust of their victims by being nice to them. They can even be romantic.

So when you approach them, be sure to check in by asking, "Is anything about my behaviour that's making you feel uncomfortable?" This helps empower them and lets them take the lead. For instance, if they tell you they need more personal space, you may need to back off a bit.

❖ **Let them make small choices**

For example, let them choose where to sit, whether you're facilitating a session for a client, or when you go out to eat or to the cinema with a friend.

- **Focus on their strengths and list them**

    Help them build resilience by getting them to focus on their strengths. This will positively reframe how they think about themselves. Encourage self-care regimes as well.

- **Establish positive goals, and break down strategies to achieve them**

    To give them purpose that's aligned to their values, teach them the tools they can use to stay positive and look after themselves.

▸ **Step four: Healing**

People who are getting over a negative experience need to have a daily healing practice tailored specifically for them.

One technique is yoga, which has been proven to be the most effective treatment to release anxiety, depression and even traumas held in the body. Van der Kolk noted that yoga is even more effective than medication in the treatment of PTSD.

For some, talking about their experiences in therapy can re-traumatise them. I believe the 'clean language' treatment, co-developed and taught by James Lawley, Penny Tompkins and (the late) David Grove, is the most effective, because it works quickly and uses a landscape of metaphors in the mind to distance them from the story of the traumas.

If you need help, get it. No matter how mild or serious your level of discomfort, something can be done. You deserve a great life if you want it, and peace is within your reach.

Another way you help people is with the Fit Mind technique. Could you explain what that is?

Much like you would exercise regularly for a healthy physique, I would recommend doing the *Fit Mind* technique, which is part of the more comprehensive eight-step empowerment program I've put together for my clients and also practise myself. Within the program we go into much more detail, but here's the framework you can implement straight away. For it to be the most effective, you need to do it daily, so go ahead and set an alarm for yourself.

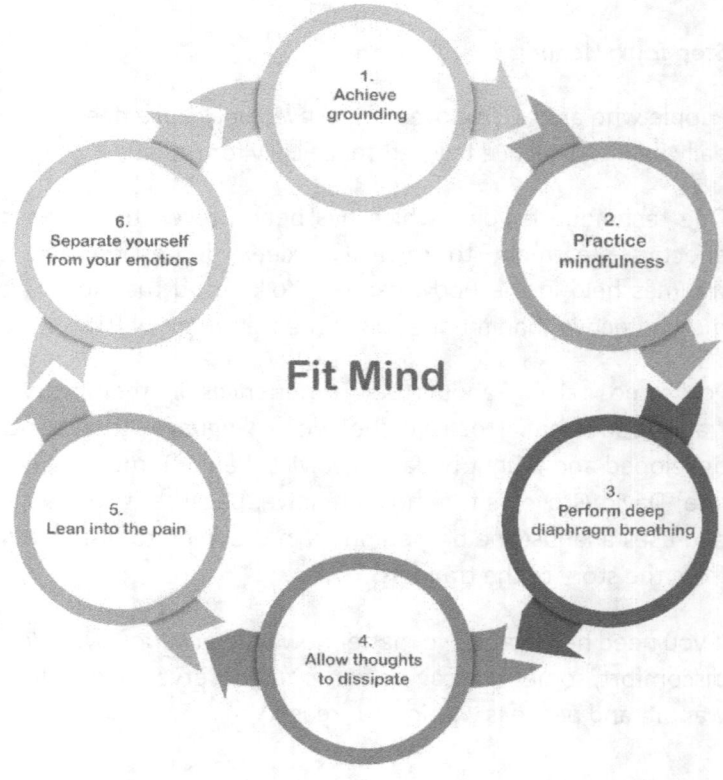

Mind Fitness

1. **Achieve grounding**

   Put both your feet on the floor. Know that you are supported by the earth. Feel it under you.

2. **Practice mindfulness**

   The most basic technique is to focus on two things you can see, hear, taste, feel and smell in the moment. Mindfulness has been scientifically proven to reduce inflammatory diseases, such as cancers.

3. **Perform deep diaphragm breathing**

   Breathe in for a count of five, hold for a moment, and then let it out slowly. Repeat five times a day. This desensitises your amygdala, the part of your brain that triggers the fight/ flight/ freeze response, until it only fires off when necessary.

4. **Allow thoughts to dissipate**

   Thoughts are just energy waves. By allowing them to dissipate, evaporate or pass by, you control whether you ride that wave and if your thought becomes a feeling that throws you into a pit of despair. Eckhart Tolle says, "People make a critical mistake of believing that what they think is what they are, and these thoughts become entities that live in their heads. These thoughts were mostly not even theirs but come from stressed parents, society and media."

5. **Lean into the pain**

   Leaning into the pain means sitting with the discomfort and not distracting yourself away from it. A great mentor told me, "True mindfulness is to be okay with whatever is happening right now, even if it isn't comfortable, and asking yourself, *Can I stay with this for one more breath?*"

6. **Separate yourself from your emotions**

   Stop labelling yourself as an anxious or angry person. Instead use language like, "I notice anxiety is around at the moment." You can then observe physical symptoms and kindly accept why they may be happening.

   Practice these every day to develop a strong mind that's fit and ready to go. The side effects are great joy and peace.

What mindset do you believe is needed to create a great life?

- Having forgiveness and self-love

- Choosing empowering thoughts as often as possible and being kind to yourself

- Focusing on gratitude and happiness

- Forgiving yourself and others you feel have wronged you or hurt those you love

I read the most beautiful take on forgiveness in the book *Calling in the One* by Katherine Woodward-Thomas. She refers to an ex-boyfriend and business partner who wronged her greatly, and while at her annual three-day ashram stay, she sat in silence and asked for help with her internal challenges. She managed to overcome all but one. She just couldn't let it go or find any way to forgive this man who'd left her and taken the business they'd built together.

On the last day, she called out to the sky in frustration and heard a voice that said, "We know he wronged you and is in great debt to you. We have taken up the debt from him and wish to repay you with equal or more, but we are not able to do this while your thoughts are still tied in hurt, anger, resentment and injustice towards him."

With that, she was able to release the disempowering feelings, and what flowed to her was abundance beyond her wildest dreams.

I've used many forgiveness processes with myself and for my clients, and I believe this is an ongoing and valuable practice. I would suggest finding a forgiveness process that works best for you.

What are your tips for getting through a difficult time in life?

Whenever my clients are experiencing a challenging time, I check if they have the foundations of eating healthy and sleeping eight hours a night, as well as reducing their alcohol intake, eliminating recreational drugs, and reviewing prescribed medications with the help of their doctors. I also recommend regular exercise. Focusing on the practical really helps in non-extreme situations and complements working with the mind.

I also believe that journaling and talking to someone about your story helps you heal. Ultimately, you need to figure out the best solution for yourself with professional assistance. Just reach out.

What is your most uplifting client story?

I'd love to share a story of a man who twelve years ago wound up homeless. He had an incredible mindset and big dreams but was riddled with past disappointments, low expectations from his community and had the biggest suitcase of guilt anyone had ever carried around, which caused massive internal conflict.

I used all of the tools I'd picked up along the way to be the best coach for him. Now he's running one of the biggest companies in his area of expertise in Sydney. He inspires a large team of people across Australia, and I believe he's destined for even more.

I tailor my practices for my clients and their individual needs, whether it's one-on-one sessions, workshops, in-person or online.

I'm driven to reaching the people who wouldn't normally be able to help themselves, and the support of my clients is what makes this a reality. I feel grateful to be able to live and teach my passion.

How will developing a strong mindset help build courage?

The greatest freedom is on the other side of your biggest fears. The worst tragedy is dying with your music still inside of you. Don't live with regrets. My advice is to take advantage of all the help available to you, practice a strong, fit mindset...and make that leap! I know it works, because every time I've felt terrified of something, I've applied these principles, and the result is greater and greater courage.

It's okay to feel fear, but in many situations, you can choose whether or not it will restrict your life.

How can someone best guarantee their success?

Whether you believe you can or believe you can't, you're right. What I know for certain is that if you choose to adjust your behaviours and outside world in a way that will help you remain in your comfort zone, so your phobias and anxieties aren't triggered, then your world will become smaller and less exciting. What isn't allowed to flourish, will die. You don't need to continue carrying suitcases of shame, guilt, hurt, anger and negative thoughts.

Practise opening your heart and mind, grow, be true to your values and trust yourself.

> "Our doubts are traitors, and make us lose the good we oft might win, by fearing to attempt."
> ~Shakespeare, Measure for Measure

Having consistency, staying healthy, practicing forgiveness and taking action are the keys to producing the results you desire.

 To discover more about how Rani can help you *Elevate Your Mindset*, simply visit www.elevatebooks.com/mindset

Peter Bliss
Mindfulness

Peter Bliss is a mindfulness and human behaviour coach, international keynote speaker and licensed Demartini facilitator. By combining ancient philosophies and science-based research such as neuroplasticity (the brain's ability to heal itself after an injury), as well as epigenetic science-based research and his own corporate experience, he helps individuals and businesses gain focus, clarity and direction.

Peter's background is in mathematics, science, psychology and marketing. He's also a certified meditation, tai chi and qigong teacher.

Prior to founding his company, Business is Bliss, he worked in senior management and marketing roles with large blue-chip multinational companies for over twenty years.

Peter is the father of five and is currently doing a master's in human behaviour.

Peter Bliss
Mindfulness

What are your biggest life lessons?

I've learnt quite a few life lessons, because the older I get, the more I'm still learning and realising there's so much I don't know.

What I do know is that I'll continue to learn for the rest of my life, and with just that attitude alone, I'll keep my brain and mental health alive and well for many years to come. My biggest lessons are best answered by a few of my all-time favourite quotes:

> "It's not what happens to you that matters, it's your perception and how you choose to react to what happens to you that matters."
>
> ~William James, The father of modern psychology.

> "If you change the way you look at things, the things you look at will change."
>
> "Things turn out best for the people who make the best out of the way things turn out."
>
> ~Art Linkletter.

Mindfulness

> "Controlling the breath is a prerequisite for controlling both the mind (thoughts) and the body."
>
> "It's your choice – Victim of history or master of destiny."
>
> ~Dr John Demartini

What does love mean to you?

Love is seeing the benefits and drawbacks to the magnificence of everything on this planet and the universe, and wisdom is how quickly it happens. As Dr John Demartini says, "It's the synthesis and synchronicity of complementary opposites."

Love also means being truly grateful for *everything* that has happened in my life up to this point, including the support and the challenges along the way and not just the 'good things'. In my later years, this has meant truly appreciating and accepting the parts of me I used to resent, or be guilty and ashamed of, such as rebelling against my Christian upbringing when I was a kid, smoking and drinking as a teenager, working for both a cigarette and an alcohol company for many years in senior roles, and getting divorced and leaving my first wife.

True love is what many theologians and philosophers recognise as the magnificent hidden order and secret workings of the divine master plan.

I believe we're all a part of that hidden order of the matrix. There are over seven billion people right now on this planet, and many are oblivious to how we're all connected with what quantum physicists call *quantum entanglement*. Albert Einstein observed and documented this over one-hundred years ago and called it "spooky action at a distance."

When you truly love people for who they are, they turn into the ones you love.

What do you think is your life purpose?

I believe we're all on this planet to grow, evolve and serve others in some way. It's just a matter of choosing and realising the form of the service. Yours might be building a business that employs people, raising a family or designing technology. It could also be in the field of dance, music or art.

My life purpose is to teach and speak internationally and locally about mindfulness, mental health and wellbeing, using the many holistic techniques I've learnt and studied on my own journey.

Everyone wants the same thing, which is to be loved and appreciated for who they are, as a unique individual with their own set of priorities.

Have you had any aha moments that changed everything for you?

I've had three pivotal aha moments that changed everything for me:

> **Aha moment number one: My first near-death experience**
>
> When I was in my early thirties, I worked in a senior sales role for a cigarette company, even though I'd given up smoking while there and hated myself for devoting my career to this industry. But I was well-paid and the only breadwinner. At that stage we already had two of our eventual four children, both under the age of seven, and a mortgage.
>
> One morning while driving to work, about five minutes into an hour-long drive, I started getting pains in my chest and tingling down my right arm. Of course, my flight, fight or freeze stress response took over, and my inner animal-panicked mind thought the worst: heart attack! I was fortunately driving past a hospital

at the time (The SAN) and had the good sense to drive in, but not enough to go straight to emergency.

Instead, I drove to the visitor car park a few hundred metres down the hill in the bush and about three-hundred steps below the entrance. As I made my way there, the pain got worse, my breathing became shorter and shallower, and I didn't think I'd make it, to be honest. By the time I did eventually get to the entrance, I was a mess, physically, mentally and emotionally.

I went up to the stunned lady at reception and sputtered, "I think I'm having a heart atta..." and collapsed in front of her. What followed was two days in intensive care, on oxygen, not knowing whether I'd had a heart attack or not. After getting a myriad of tests, I was diagnosed with a virus called *Pericarditis*, which has all of the exact same symptoms as a heart attack but is a virus of the pericardium, which is the muscle surrounding the heart. I was told to take some pills and a few days off, and I would be fine.

I remember being quite relieved, and especially loved the long label for my condition. After a few weeks I was back doing the same thing: working too hard, hating myself for being at a cigarette company and worrying too much in my head, while keeping my fears and anxieties inside. After all, I was a typical Aussie bloke.

But what I did do was secretly experiment with some techniques, which in the mid-eighties were considered alternative and weird. I went to a retreat called Camp Eden on the Gold Coast hinterland and tried massage, rebirthing, yoga and meditation, and I dipped in and out of these practices for the next ten years.

I frequented Camp Eden when I needed to escape from my life. I'd get a week of recharge before coming back to Sydney and getting back into it again: the pressures...the stress...the rat race.

Peter Bliss

▸ **Aha moment number two: My second near-death experience**

With this one I did 'wake up' and change my life dramatically. The catalyst was another episode of heart attack symptoms ten years later, which occurred when I was at Camp Eden Retreat in a cabin by myself. After spending a week there, I was meant to be going home, but I didn't want to go back to my corporate life. I hated it. I was scared to death of it, and it nearly took my life away, literally and physically.

I was thinking all of this at about 2am, lying in bed, when I started having the pain in my chest and the tingling down my arm again, but it was much worse and way more intense than the first one ten years before. I really thought this was it, and I was so frightened and frozen with fear, I couldn't move. My breath became shallower and shorter, and I panicked, but I remained on the bed literally watching my breath and life leave me, until I eventually passed out, believing this was my death. The last thing I remember thinking was that this must have been what my father had experienced just before he died of a heart attack at age fifty-seven, thirteen years previous.

I didn't die, obviously, but I saw the darkness, a light at the end of a tunnel and a voice I'm certain was my father's, telling me all I had to do was start breathing again. I remember consciously taking short sips of air, and when I did come to I was still lying there, focusing on breathing slowly, until each breath became longer and deeper. It was a lengthy process, but I managed to regain my control...my thoughts...and my life. When I was able to move again and regained enough strength to get up, I went to find help.

I was admitted to John Flynn hospital on the Gold Coast Queensland in intensive care.

Again, after another two days of testing, including an ultrasound, an angiogram and many others, I was told there was nothing wrong with me. All the tests were okay.

So at that point my big *aha* came while I was lying there contemplating my life and the absolute terror and fear I'd experienced before I 'died', as well as what I now had to go back and face in Sydney, with my corporate rat-race life.

There I was on a Saturday morning, lying in hospital 1000km away from where I was supposed to start a new job as a general manager of a company on Monday morning. I was also scheduled to begin lecturing part-time at UTS and had promised to take my kids to an international football game the next day.

Just thinking about all of this started my worry cycle again, and I could immediately feel my whole body tense up. My pulse quickened, and my heart pounded faster. I pushed the red panic nurse button, and when a sister came in I told her I wasn't feeling well. She took my pulse and blood pressure, and to no surprise, discovered they were both elevated, so she left to get me some more medication.

Then came my big aha moment: I was causing my blood pressure to rise and my pulse to race just from my thoughts.

My solution was to test my hypothesis. I got out of bed and sat in the chair next to it. Then I closed my eyes and practised some of the simple breathing and meditation techniques I'd learnt over the last years at Camp Eden but hadn't been practicing daily. After five minutes of slowing and deepening my breathing and focusing on it, I knew I'd changed my physiology.

I got back into bed, pressed the red panic button again and asked the same sister to take my vitals while informing her I was fine now and didn't need the medication. And guess what? Everything was normal again that quickly. This is when a light bulb went on inside of me, and I knew the true power of the connection between the mind and body. Yes, I'd been wiggling my toes consciously my whole life, but this was something much more profound. My intention, my perceptions, my thoughts, my breath and my reactions, were all keys to my physiology.

This whole experience led me to eventually leave the corporate world I'd been in for thirty years and start my own business, focusing on speaking, teaching, coaching and running retreats about the mind-body connection, which I've been doing since 2005.

▶ **Aha moment number three: My sister's suicide in 2012**

On the 27th of January 2012, my big sister Diana committed suicide in Perth at age fifty-seven. She was only twenty months older than I was, and though she lived the last thirty years of her life either in Perth or overseas in London and New York, we were still close.

She was a successful Tony-award-nominated theatre producer and married to a jailed fraudster, millionaire Perth businessman and America's Cup winner, Alan Bond.

In 2011 she was living in London and had attempted suicide twice. Both times I'd dropped everything and flown over from Sydney to try and help her. She was "clinically depressed" and suffering from "acute anxiety", while struggling to function day to day. She was in and out of clinics, and at my urging she eventually sectioned into a mental health facility in London.

While her suicide was an absolute tragedy at the time, it has, in hindsight, become a high *aha* moment for me, as well as a critical point in my future growth and understanding of mental health and wellbeing.

The knowledge and wisdom I've gained since Di's death has changed my life, and the lives of many of my clients. It led me to the world of Dr John Demartini and his profound Demartini method and grief technique, which I've combined with my revolutionary mindfulness practices in my teaching, speaking and workshops, as well as my work with individuals and groups.

Why do you think so many people are overwhelmed and unhappy in life?

People compare their current life and reality to someone else's reality and set unrealistic expectations for themselves about where they "should" be. This means they don't have a clear vision of where they want to be and/or don't have a strategy or congruent plan as to how to get there, that's aligned to what's important to them.

They're addicted to what many 'self-help gurus' preach about always being happy and positive and buy into the television and magazine fantasy.

Also, many people are highly focused on digital gadgets. This can cause less human touch and interactions. In this day and age, people have to process everything quickly and aren't paying full attention to every piece of their life due to multi-tasking, but the brain isn't designed that way.

People spend days moving from one thing to another and doing nothing properly or mindfully, only paying partial attention to everything.

All human beings are meant to experience life in all its glory, and sometimes gory, detail.

What's needed is more mindfulness, which means paying attention in a particular way on purpose, in the present moment, without judgement.

Life isn't about getting someplace else. It's about consciously being where you already are and realising the full power and potential of your awareness and presence right now, in this moment.

What do you think people's biggest life issues are?

In my experience, it's that some people have a tendency to get stuck in what psychologists might refer to as 'animal', or lower-mind, behaviour, also known as reptilian brain. It means looking for instant gratification and avoiding pain, while seeking pure pleasure.

While stuck in this stress response, they may need to get a quick dopamine fix, whether it's from sugar, caffeine, chocolate, alcohol, drugs or sex, that provides an instant reward and leads to short-term gratification. Looking for 'happiness' and 'positivity' all the time, while remaining in a constant state of fight, flight or freeze, leads to a state of not being present at all.

By going from one distraction to the next, you won't take full responsibility for your own personal wellbeing and wind up remaining up in your head, having worrying thoughts and constant distractions while trying to multi-task. What you may not realise is that you have the power to jump off the stress and anxiety train and get in touch with how your whole body, mind and soul work together to give feedback as to what's truly happening. This opens up the potential of the most evolved and higher mind.

Due to a lack of knowledge about how to get in touch with your own vision, creativity, intuition, solutions and imagination, you may look to others to feel happy and complete. The result will be an inability to tap into your own enthusiasm, gratitude and presence, and you'll never understand that happiness is an inside job, dependent upon your inner condition.

I lived this way for much of my life, and I learnt the hard way where this type of long-term imbalanced perspective can lead.

How do you help people with this issue within your practice?

I'm one of the few in the world who teaches both mindfulness and the work of Dr John Demartini.

Through a range of mindfulness-based techniques, including *tai chi* and meditation, you can reduce your stress and experience a whole new world of awareness, growth and development, which will improve your ability to remain calm in difficult circumstances.

How did you become interested in mindfulness, mental health and the whole mind-body connection?

I've always wanted to know the answers to the big question: *Why and what are we here for?* Growing up in small NSW country towns and being the son of a Methodist and Uniting church minister, exposed me to one view of some of the big questions and answers, but I always wanted to know more.

Even when I started working at the bottom in sales with large companies, I wanted to know why the marketing departments gave us certain instructions regarding our sales campaigns.

I eventually received a post-graduate marketing degree and got a job in marketing, which led to needing to understand the company's strategy. Over time realised I had a desire to run the company, and I eventually did. That's when I started to have issues with stress and tried all sorts of tools and techniques to overcome it. I've even travelled to a little village in South America and visited a miracle man there called 'John of God' to try and find answers. Then when my big sister Di committed suicide, I continued my search with renewed focus.

Do you have an approach to Mindfulness?

My approach to mindful living, fulfilment and contentment is based on the 7 secrets to mindfulness, mindful leadership, wholeness and authentic wellness. I call them The 7L's. They're the basis for my workshops and presentations, as well as my teaching and corporate speaking engagements. I'm happy to share the basics of them here:

1. Lighten up—with gratitude

As Jim Stephens says, "Cultivate an attitude of gratitude." This doesn't just mean appreciating all the 'good' things in life. True, authentic gratitude means also being grateful for the challenges in life, big and small, that have enabled you to become resilient, evolve and grow into the person you are today.

There are three medical reasons why laughing and smiling are good for you:

- It lowers your blood pressure

- Cortisol (the stress hormone) is lowered immediately

- The immune system works better, which produces more SIGA, an antivirus fighter.

- Do simple gratitude meditations every day. Here's one simple technique to do when you first wake up.

    o Get out of bed and sit in a chair.

    o Set your alarm for eight minutes.

    o Stay still and think about all the things in your life you have to be grateful for. Focus on your chest and heart, while breathing into your chest with long, slow deep breaths.

Even if you have a busy schedule, make time every morning for this technique. It's a nice way to start the day.

2. **Let go**

   Holding on to emotional stuff like fears, resentment, anger, guilt and shame, isn't good for anyone. Most people won't let go of stuff, because they don't know how to. The only techniques that truly work are having a simple daily mindfulness practice such as *qigong*, meditation, yoga, *tai chi*, and simple, slow-breathing techniques that will dissolve your emotional baggage and neuroplasticically, alter your perceptions and literally change your brain.

   Shaking is a powerful, effective *qigong* technique you should practice every day. It can strengthen and detoxify cells through the quick, extra force each shake places on them. Shaking relaxes and warms all of the muscles, organs, joints and fascia of the body. Lymph flow is enhanced, and your immune function improves. Your blood flow increases, and hormonal secretions benefit your skin.

3. **Loosen Up**

   To quote Ralph Waldo Emerson, "Our soul calls us to even greater circles, but the mind, with its belief systems, hems us in". Limiting beliefs about self are what hold most people back from achieving their full potential. If you're not convinced by now that learning and practicing mindfulness is a good idea, below are the words of Harvard neuroscience researchers in the *Harvard Business Review*:

   "Mindfulness should no longer be considered a "nice to have". It's a "must have"; a way to keep our brains healthy, to support self-regulation and effective decision-making capabilities, and to protect ourselves from toxic stress".

You can loosen up physically through gentle exercises, mentally through various meditation, focussing and breathing techniques, and emotionally through asking questions that balance your imbalanced perceptions.

The best definition of mindfulness is paying attention in a particular way, in the present moment, without judgement. A tight, stiff, stuck, body and physiology is the result of a tight, stiff, stuck mind, perception and thought pattern.

4. **Learn to listen to your innermost dominant thought**

According to research, everyone has between 40,000 and 70,000 thoughts every day, and on average, seventy-five percent of these are negative. So how do you learn to let go of them all and focus on the dominant ones?

Your thoughts are just thoughts. They're real but not the truth. They're part of you but not the whole of you. By learning to just observe them as a witness, you can learn to let them go if they're not serving you. Listen to your intuition, your creativity, your decisions, your solutions and your vision.

You're probably not even aware of your inner world, because you rely on the outside for contentment and happiness. You think you'll finally be happy if you get that job, acquire that shiny new car, attract the perfect partner or build your dream home. Most of the 'thoughts' you pay attention to aren't the real innermost dominant ones. They're what the Dalai Lama refers to as *the monkey mind*, which is constant negative self-talk. But through practice, you'll quickly learn to be aware of your real and most dominant thoughts.

Mindfulness

5. Learn to breathe

If you suffer from long-term stress, you may have turned into a short, shallow, mouth breather without realising how it's minimising your potential and daily performance.

By deepening, lengthening and controlling your breathing on a regular basis, you can change your life.

Pranayama is one yogic breathing practice that can help. Prana means the life force or breath sustaining the body, and ayama is 'to extend or draw out'. There's also diaphragmatic, or belly, breathing, which involves contracting the diaphragm. Air enters the lungs, the chest rises and the belly expands.

Breathing is the key to life. It sounds so simple, but if you practice these simple daily practices, you can greatly improve your energy levels.

Most people don't use their full lung capacity because they're not breathing slowly and deeply enough. You might go for days not being aware that you're holding your breath and breathing short and shallow. There's an old Zen saying that everyone has the same number of breaths, it just depends on how quickly you use them.

6. Learn to be present

With more awareness of your self, your breath, and your innermost dominant thoughts, you'll experience more moments of presence.

When you're doing what really matters to you, you'll already be disciplined, reliable, focused and present. If you're doing what's important to someone else, you'll be easily distracted, and you'll procrastinate, hesitate and get frustrated. So presence is a skill you can learn through either daily mindfulness practice or by doing and focusing on what's really important to you.

7. Learn to take responsibility for self

Only by taking responsibility for everything that's happening to you, including your reaction to the outer world, can your life begin to change. You're the common denominator. Yes, you may have some influence on everything around you, but all you can change are your perceptions, decisions and actions, so focus on these. Everything and everyone else is out of your control.

How did you decide on the name and logo for your business?

I'm grateful to my father, The Reverend Douglas Walter Bliss, who was a minister from Bathurst NSW, for passing down his family name to me. Most people, when they hear me speak or experience my teaching, think I made up my surname.

Having spent most of my life in the corporate world in senior positions, working for large multi-national companies, I have a thorough understanding of corporations and how they operate at all levels. I started at the bottom and worked my way to the top at a young age, and I actually registered the company name, *Business is Bliss*, long before I started my own existing business in 2005.

My belief is that whether working in someone else's business or your own, it's your choice whether you're doing what you love or loving what you do, and whether to view and perceive your current work situation or career as on your way to success, or in the way of it. I certainly used to always think that whatever I was doing, whether as a sales rep supervisor, manager or managing director, as being 'in the way' at the time I was in those roles. I was unfulfilled and discontented.

Looking back now, with wisdom and hindsight, I can see that those roles were actually on the way to where I am right now in my own business and life. They were perfect training ground for what I do, which is to coach, teach and speak to people at all levels in companies of all sizes.

Mindfulness

I help people create wellbeing, innovation and improved productivity in the workplace by teaching them to have a greater sense of purpose and meaning. My teachings include practical strategies for stress reduction, minimising conflict when dealing with distractions and easing fatigue.

How do you start your day?

1. I start every day with my gratitude and mindfulness practice. Since it's still dark, I light a candle before beginning the process. First, I complete a seated body scan, yoga *nidra* style, gratitude meditation for twenty minutes, which is the length of my CD. Most days it leads me to tears of inspiration for what I have to appreciate in my life.

2. I do a twenty-minute *qigong* meditation and some *qigong* self-massage for ten.

3. I complete four Golden Wheel *Qigong* exercises for either fifteen or thirty minutes.

4. I complete the five Tibetans (yoga postures) for thirteen minutes.

5. I do my own "Bliss Routine" of yoga and breathing for twenty-five minutes.

If I have time, I then do a mindful walk in bush for up to an hour. I also drink lemon juice squeezed into water.

I'm grateful to do this, because I work from home and live near a beautiful national park while only being twenty minutes from Sydney.

Is meditation or mindfulness something everyone should practice?

Yes, I believe so. It saved my life, and I believe it can save anyone's.

How does someone keep inspired on a daily basis?

Do what you love through delegation, or love what you do through linking. Perform the inner work. Have a daily mindfulness practice. Connect every day with your body, mind and spirit, and practise being grateful for what is, even through life's challenges. Inspiration is internal and intrinsic. It's latent in most people and is an untapped resource.

I can help you transform your life, lead you down a different path and give you some unique, powerful alternatives. Please visit my website to find out more at businessisbliss.com.au.

 To discover more about how Peter can help you *Elevate Your Mindset*, simply visit www.elevatebooks.com/mindset

Rebecca Fox

Mindset and Meaning

Rebecca Fox is an executive coach with over eighteen years of experience dedicated to helping her clients uncover, create and live their most authentic life.

She's assisted thousands of people to win their dream job, uncover their true calling, successfully negotiate their salary, rebound from redundancy and master their world of work, regardless of their experience. She's conducted over 8,000 business, career and coaching sessions and has been the recipient of multiple awards for excellence.

Rebecca has held leadership positions in Fortune 500 companies and continues to be a popular speaker within her industry, as well as university forums. Today, Rebecca continues to directly impact the lives of thousands of people from across the world through her firm, *OneFox Consulting*.

Rebecca Fox
Mindset and Meaning

What's your biggest life lesson?

The most impacting lesson I've learned so far, is that *you don't need permission to be successful*. The pathways to success differ for everyone, but my entry ticket is no less valid than it was for Bill Gates, Richard Branson, Serena Williams or Heidi Klum…and neither is yours.

As I realised this truth, I also began to understand the genuine power of *mindset* and *meaning*. This was in no way a new concept, of course, but it was new to me, and I was fascinated by it. I started asking myself questions about how long these ideas had been around and why I was only just learning about them.

How long has Mindset been around as a concept?

It's hard to know exactly, but the Greek philosopher, Epíktētos, born in approximately 50AD, was one of the first philosophers to establish ideas surrounding the importance of mindset. What he said was that while we will never be able to completely control or choose our external circumstances, what is within our control is the *meaning* we choose to apply in response, as well as our mindset, which determines the success of our reactions. In other words, what happens to us isn't important; it's how we react to it that shapes our lives.

Have you had a big aha moment that changed your life?

For a time I was convinced that success was only reserved for the *lucky few,* those with *special talents and gifts*, or the truly smart. In other words, people who weren't me. My brother and I are both adopted. He has a genius IQ and was celebrated and acknowledged for his scientific and mathematical prowess. Because he won almost every academic school prize, he helped to reinforce my ideas about who deserved success.

My father also placed a greater value on subjects like math and science, as opposed to the arts. I vividly remember fishing for a compliment from him when I was sixteen, as I'd topped the grade in English with a poem I'd written. His response to me was, "Yes, but English is a soft subject, so it doesn't really count now, does it"?

My dear dad's comment was merely a reflection of a widely adopted belief structure that was echoed by the schools I'd attended, where there would be four times as many prizes available for math and science stars as for drama and art prodigies. But what I didn't realise at the time was that:

▸ My dad's limited belief structure fostered a fixed mindset ideology.

▸ These limiting beliefs in no way had to be mine.

My aha moment came when I realised my dad was full of a **B**elief **S**ystem (BS) I didn't subscribe to. In fact, I believed him to be wrong.

What do you mean by a fixed mindset?

A fixed mindset is one that heralds the belief that intelligence or talent are fixed traits and can't be manipulated. So, my dad's fixed mindset meant he truly believed I would never be successful in any of the 'real' academic disciplines. This doesn't mean he loved me any less. In fact, he was an amazing father. However, it was impossible for him to believe I could learn a talent or become smart.

People with a fixed mindset place enormous value on documenting their intelligence or talent, as opposed to developing them from the ground up. Carol Dweck, the psychologist who coined the modern term 'mindset', notes that 'fixed mindsetters' believe that talent alone, devoid and free of effort, creates success.

On the opposite side is a growth mindset.

In a growth mindset, it's believed that all of your skills and abilities can be developed through perseverance and persistence, and that your IQ and talent are merely the foundations from which you flourish or grow. People with a growth mindset have a thirst for knowledge and a passion to study and discover. A growth mindset also promotes tenacity and resilience, which are essential for abundance and success.

How did you develop a growth mindset in an environment with such fixed mindset ideas?

The first thing I had to do was stop seeking approval. By prioritising approval over learning, I was forfeiting my own potential for growth.

Even though I always knew I was loved, little I achieved seemed to please or impress my parents. Throwaway remarks such as the one my dad made about my poem began seeping into my psyche and took on the meaning that academically I wasn't bright, and what I chose to pursue didn't really count. That while I did try hard, I wasn't gifted or particularly talented and university or higher learning would be beyond me. However, this didn't stop me from desperately seeking my parents' approval and permission to be successful and to count for something worthwhile in their eyes.

In my final year of school, I decided to go out for chairperson of the school board, which was like being school captain. If successful, I would be the first female student in the history of the school to ever hold the honorary position. The representative had to exemplify academic aptitude equally across the sciences and the arts, as well as exhibit social responsibility and public spirit. The result would be determined by a student vote.

I worked hard. I was passionate. I'd learned much about government educative legislation and the bureaucratic responsibilities of a school board, even though I was positive I couldn't win. I put together a sound campaign, rallied my supporters and in the end had the privilege of gaining their votes. I won the election and raced home to share the news.

My mother's immediate reaction wasn't to congratulate me or celebrate my hard-earned title, but rather she jumped in the car and raced off to the principal's office to demand the title be revoked. At the time, my mother and I were in the midst of a 'colourful' adolescent journey, due primarily to my growth mindset clashing with her fixed one. She vehemently felt this position would serve to feed my challenging disposition.

When she returned, she told me I was 'very lucky' indeed that the position had been won through a democratic process, so the principal couldn't revoke it.

This was my turning point moment as a young adult. It just didn't seem right. Most parents I knew were so proud of their kids when they were voted school captain or prefect, and here I was, chairperson of the school board, and there was no recognition.

Nevertheless, it also served as a gift. I realised, for the first time in my life, that I didn't need permission or approval to be successful, as that would be casting myself as the perpetual victim in my own story.

I was just seventeen when it dawned on me that I had a choice as to how I interpreted and internalised the meaning of my mother's reactions. I realised it had nothing to do with me and everything to do with her and her need to be the best. Sorrow and anguish doesn't come from what happens to you. It comes from the stories you tell yourself about the adversity and hardships that will happen as a result of the meaning you give to a particular situation. You can't choose your external circumstances, but you can always choose how you react and respond to them.

I may not have had my brother's IQ, but I had a way of looking at the world that I believed was just as valuable, if not more so. I had a good work ethic, determination, a love of learning and a passion to become the best version of myself I could be. I didn't believe I had to be born with talent to excel. In fact, my own short experience had proven the exact opposite was true.

My *growth mindset* served to ensure my financial independence, supported me through university and ensured that in my first-ever job I not only won numerous accolades for excellence, but was earning a six-figure salary. To some that may be a measure of success. All I know is that I didn't need permission from anyone else but myself to get there. When I stopped seeking approval, I began to flourish.

What are some examples of other ways to cultivate a growth mindset?

- **Use the word *yet***

    When struggling with a task, you need to tell yourself you haven't mastered it *yet*. This assumes a potential future positive.

- **Develop a sense of purpose**

    Keep the big picture in mind.

- **Recognise and embrace your inadequacies and shortcomings**

    Hiding from your weaknesses means you'll never overcome them.

- **Celebrate your learnings and growth**

    Share your progress and experience with others throughout your journey, and not just the end result.

- **Value growth over speed**

    Learning fast isn't the same as learning well, and learning well can take time, during which you might make mistakes.

- **Recognise and reward actions, not traits**

    For example, praising your child for doing something intelligent and not their intelligence.

- **See criticism as a positive**

    Feedback is a gift, regardless of its flavour.

- **Cultivate grit**

    Dweck's work showed that students with that extra bit of determination will be more likely to seek approval from themselves, rather than look externally for it.

How did you become interested in mindset?

I became interested in mindset when I first learned about the ideas surrounding manifestation, also known as the law of attraction. In the late nineties I was sitting in my doctor's waiting room and picked up one of those trashy magazines that are always sitting there. Amidst the glossy fashion photos and advice columns like, 'What To Do If You Suspect He's Cheating' and 'How To Lose 10kg in 10 Days'. I stumbled upon 'The Powers of Manifestation', and with a mixture of scepticism and intrigue, I read it.

I recall the writer boasting about her ability to not only manifest a 'rock star carpark' in any crowded street, but also how she'd successfully manifested the very car she was driving when looking for such a coveted space. Though the piece left me doubting the author's intent and authenticity, it didn't necessarily detract from the wider theme I'd been contemplating for some time.

Through my studies of philosophy, I'd come across the principles pertaining to *the law of attraction*, which seemed to parallel the ideas behind manifestation. The theory is that *wherever you focus your thoughts, you bring positive or negative experiences into your life*.

Newton had coined a similar theory in 1686. He stated that every action has an equal and opposite reaction. In physics, this means that when an object collides with a target, there's an equal force going into and away from the target, or more simply put: cause and effect.

I thought to myself, *Are they suggesting that If I merely think of something positive, I will attract something positive, and vice-versa? Could it be this simple?*

I decided to do a little further investigation and discovered that the law of karma applies a broad view of Newton's law beyond just physical motion. It says that when a person applies a force on another part of life, that force will go into its intended target, but it will also return to the person.

Though I never excelled in math or physics, I was more comfortable living an existence that lent its faith to science and math over karma and religious ideas like those of the Buddhist tradition. But then I realised they might actually be borrowing from one another, or maybe they were both lending commentary on an equally experiential observation.

Newton and Einstein had proved to me that even if I really, truly believed in my heart that I could fly, jumping off a cliff would send me plummeting to my death, no matter how much energy I put into believing otherwise.

Realising that my digging was now leading me into a more religious realm, I sought the opinion of a great friend of mine who was devout in his Christian faith.

I asked him if he'd heard of this idea of manifestation, and if so what his opinion of it was. His response surprised me. He was astonished I hadn't already heard about it and shared his point of view from a religious perspective, which to me, a non-church-goer, sounded the same as Newton's law, karma and the law of attraction.

He recited a couple of quotes from the Bible. Such as Mark 11:24: *Whatever you ask for in prayer, believe that you have received it, and it will be yours* and Mathew 7:7: *Ask, and it will be given to you; seek, and you will find; knock, and it will be opened to you.* Not to bias his response, he also quoted the opening theme from *Monkey Magic*.... *"'Tathagata Buddha,' the Father Buddha said. 'With our thoughts, we make the world.'"*

Growing up in the eighties, we both loved *Monkey Magic*, but I couldn't help thinking that while manifestation was touted at the time as the *zeitgeist* of new-age philosophy, it wasn't new or original in concept. Could all of these ancient, philosophical, scientific and religious beliefs be on to something after all?

Though I very much appreciated existential thinking and enjoyed the privilege of a rounded education that included religion, I wasn't a practicing participant. But because of the new questions I was asking myself, and the research I'd done, I decided to put manifestation to the test and be my own personal white mouse. What I discovered and personally experienced astounded me.

I learned that when I set my mind to a specific predetermined goal, I would achieve it. By lasering my focus and having a growth mindset, along with fierce determination and a strong belief in what I was going for, the universe would conspire to help me, and everything would come together.

What does manifestation mean to you?

For me, manifestation is simply a heightened form of goal setting, or to be more accurate, an acute form through which you shape successful outcomes.

Today I continue to practice manifestation. Though I have so much more to learn, I've enjoyed tremendous success thus far.

Some personal examples of manifested outcomes have included financial windfalls, holidays, investment properties, new business ventures, health, fitness and wellbeing, and yes, even a new car. I guess I shouldn't have been so cynical about that article after all.

What does the art of communication have to do with manifestation?

Having now expanded my mind to the opportunities of abundance and experiencing firsthand the universal response, which I *still* try to scientifically rationalise, I began to further explore how daily unconscious choices had the potential to transform into conscious ones and shape everyday life.

While harbouring my fascination with philosophy, I wanted to investigate my passion regarding the art of communication and meaning, and the impact that word choice, phrase formation and tonality could have on an outcome, which is similar to Dweck's emphasis on the word 'yet'.

I'd always been interested in etymology, which is the study of the origin of words, and the way in which their meanings have changed throughout history. I'd taken a course in linguistics at university and spoke French, Italian, German and Greek at varying levels of fluency.

While working in recruitment, a highly competitive and cutthroat environment, I came to understand the true power of mindset and communication. After listening to candidate job seekers and their choice of vernacular during the interviewing process, I realised their success in winning their desired job had little to do with their skill-set in the field, but rather their narrative and the way they communicated. For example:

- Did they successfully pepper their responses with language that evoked certainty?
- Did they use the word "I" instead of "we", such as "I was responsible for XYZ" and not "*We* were..."?
- Did they structure their narrative to indicate they were running towards the job opportunity and not away from their present or previous environment?
- Did they understand their nonverbal cues, and were they communicating them in a way that best served their desired outcomes?

The answer, at least seventy percent of the time, was *no*!

I wondered how it could be that most of my amazing candidates, who were far more learned than I was, with their PhDs, DRs and MBAs, didn't understand the impact and power of their habitual unconscious word choices, which resulted in not getting that raise or winning the job.

I knew that their decision to change and employ a purpose-driven and specific vocabulary would not only guarantee winning upward of ninety-five percent of the positions they strove for, but would also revolutionise the way they experienced the world and how they lived. This wouldn't have to be something they worked on for months. I believed that once they learned how, they would be able to immediately reap the benefits and experience the power of deliberate and conscious communication choices.

As a result of discovering how few people understood this concept, regardless of the letters that followed their name, I became devoted to coaching, consulting and sharing my findings with my candidates. They in turn not only won the jobs they sought, but went on to work in leadership positions and continued to invite me to consult and coach across their personal and professional journeys.

I was working with first-time job seekers, return-to-work moms, those transitioning careers or needing to rebound from redundancy and women wanting assistance in negotiating salary or pay rises. Though I was still predominately working within the function of 'talent acquisition', I was simultaneously helping my clients uncover, create and live their most authentic lives and consciously choose their futures while fostering a growth mindset.

Can people really manifest their own success? And if so, how?

Absolutely! Manifesting your own success starts with understanding what you want and unashamedly going for it. Hitting the target is impossible if you don't know where or what you're aiming for.

So manifesting success must start with your definition of what it is. There's no right or wrong. There's only what it looks, feels, and even smells and tastes like. Get to a place where you can describe, in intense detail, every little aspect of it, including why achieving your goal is important to you and the value and meaning you attach to your *why*. As Dr John Demartini says, *"When the voice and the vision on the inside is more profound, and more clear and loud than all opinions on the outside, you've begun to master your life."*

Discovering your vision and future belonging, are the first steps in manifesting any successful outcome. Though I unwittingly employed such practices on my own nearly twenty years previous, there was a lot of hit and miss, and perhaps unnecessary emotional turmoil along the way.

I believe it would have been exceptionally beneficial to have been coached through the process in order to hack my result more efficiently.

If you have a specific result or future in mind, I couldn't recommend a coach more strongly in this area.

Can you use this process for personal relationships, too?

Absolutely. Goal setting is goal setting.

A great example is when I was casually working with a friend of mine who'd been out of a relationship for the previous five years and was lamenting that she would never be able to find a life partner.

I said I agreed, because if she believed this to be true, it would be her reality.

Fast forward a few hours later during a coaching session, where she specifically described *not* who her perfect man was going to be, but what kind of life she wanted and the person *she* desired to be.

Some of the questions she asked and answered about herself included:

- Where do I see myself in the next ten years?
- Where am I living?
- Who is in my life partner?
- Do I have children?
- Who am I for this person?
- How do I light them up and support them?
- How do I show them my commitment?

- How do I show them economic security and companionship?
- How am I my partner's friend and also his passionate lover?
- How do I inspire my partner?
- When will I meet him?
- What year will I be married?
- What year will I fall pregnant?

Social media has created a fabricated world of relationship utopias, where everything looks shiny and perfect. My friend had been stuck in this fixed mindset, so it was no wonder she hadn't found success. This idealised version of life generates concepts like trying to make yourself look perfect and expecting your partner to be perfect as well.

It becomes about what you're getting instead of what you can contribute. The very minute my friend amended the glossy idealistic lies, adopted a growth mindset and took responsibility for her future, she began to experience power and freedom, because there's power in responsibility.

Within twenty-four months of our coaching session, she'd not only successfully attracted exactly the type of partner she could love and support, and who in return could equally show up for her, but she was married and expecting!

Accepting the responsibility for your future is the only way to create and set your specific goals, respond to them and successfully manifest them.

If you were speaking to your younger self, what advice would you give her?

I would tell myself....

Don't shy away from the F-word. In fact, the more comfortable you become with it, the more successful you will be.

I am of course talking about...*failure.*

F.A.I.L. is just a **F**irst **A**ttempt **I**n **L**earning, and only through discovering what doesn't work, will you learn what does. Falling down when you're learning to walk is the only road to running.

And hey, you don't need to seek approval to be successful. Though you'll learn this lesson at sixteen, you owe it to yourself to champion this same message daily to ensure its fortification.

Go all the way!

Understand that by jumping all in, you could lose your mother, as well as your most precious and treasured relationships, and wind up doubting all you know. Or worse yet, you could get stuck in your head so bad it feels like you're losing your mind. Just know that giving it all you've got will serve as a measure of your resilience, grit, and mindset, and will act as a mirror reflecting back how much you really want to achieve your goal.

Cultivate GRIT! You must live this life with all the intensity you can, celebrating your failures as an essential part of being alive. A life with no failures would be a life less lived, and making friends with your greatest failures and fears is the only good fight there is.

Do you have a self-defeating voice, and if so, do you have any tools to conquer it?

Yes, I do!

I've found that it's all too easy to self-sabotage. For that internal doubting voice to sneak back into my head. Just when I think she's gone for good... *POP*...there she is again.

Sure, she starts off quiet, but then, slowly and surreptitiously, she creeps back in and adjusts her volume upward. So to keep her at bay, and conquer any negative undertones, I must ensure my internal narrative is stronger, more positive and more supportive than any non-serving whisper.

I personify this voice by calling her, *Beck the Champion*. I think of her as my own personal cheerleader. She has my back in those moments when I may not be the best representative for myself. I need her, because deep down, in that dark place no one really likes to talk about, lives her nemesis. *Beck the Handbag*. I know! Crazy name, right? Maybe I called her that because she's representative of my personal baggage; that part of me that's afraid if I'm truly successful, people won't like me.

My logical self knows this is a fallacy, as there's an abundance of evidence to suggest otherwise. I feel so privileged and grateful for the support my friends and new family give me, and how my clients share that working with me has served to inspire and motivate them to make changes they'd never dreamed possible.

But still I struggle with my teenage psyche. The one that bought into a narrative that I was a mistake to begin with. How I was rejected by my birth mother and again by my adopted mother. The better I did, and the more success I received, the more rejection I seemed to experience from the people I loved.

Here's the truth, though: It takes discipline and commitment to keep those doubting voices away, but it is possible to quickly reduce the volume and eventually abolish them.

Beck the Champion is my way of managing my fear when it comes over for a visit. She'll say, *"Oh, hi, Fear. How you going? Sorry we can't stop and chat. I know you're just trying to help me out, but you're not needed right now."* She doesn't try to ignore the fear. Instead, she politely acknowledges and befriends it in order to take back control and redirect me to excitement, anticipation and fun.

One of the best real-world applications to master self-doubt is a technique known as Discovery Writing or Affirmation Journaling. This is where, on a daily basis, you take the time to hand write in a notebook or journal all the reasons why you deserve love, financial freedom, or to grow your business and be the most successful in your chosen industry.

This process will elicit a complex interaction of physical and mental processes that involves cooperation among your brain's cognitive, motor and emotion areas, right down through the brain stem and the spinal cord, culminating with it coming out of your hands and onto the paper.

There's no hack for this exercise, so banging away on the laptop isn't going to get the same result. Physically writing it out increases activity in the brain's motor cortex to manipulate your result.

In harnessing this practice, you're almost reprogramming your subconscious thoughts to serve you positively. The function, in and of itself, doesn't discriminate the data it programs, so you must ensure that it's deliberate and positive.

Primary schools have been on to this neat trick for years, which is why handwriting the same phrase over and over, such as, *I will not be disrespectful in class*, used *to be* common practice when a kid received detention. This wasn't just a punishment. It was an effective reprogramming task of their subconscious self.

Every evening before I go to sleep, I take ten minutes to write my lines to keep *Beck the Handbag* at bay. To some this may seem masochistic, or even a bit crazy, but scientific evidence also backs this practice. Research shows that journaling can help fight depression, require fewer doctor visits and lead to a healthier immune system.

People with a fixed mindset fear mostly how they will be judged by others, and even how they judge themselves. However, retaining control, moving forward and focusing on learning are characteristics of a growth mindset. *Beck the Champion* prompts me to be a learner. We both know that to fulfil our potential, we must think differently and realise we're not defined or shackled to any preconceived ideas of capability.

When you determine that you can change your own abilities and have a growth mindset, you create an 'uplift' and a new story. To quote PhD and clinical psychologist, Carl Greer, *'Change your story, change your life.'* You must understand that failing is a part of growth, so when you stumble, you must find a way to get back up again. After experiencing a setback, attach a meaning to it that will serve you, so you can get back up and have another go.

What can people do to develop a growth mindset?

Learn everything you can and put it into practice. A great option is to get a coach, which is probably the fastest way to achieve a result.

What my clients have discovered is that you can either learn to overcome challenges or succumb to them.

Life has numerous challenges in store for everyone; some expected, some unexpected, while others are merely speed bumps or a brick wall. The mindset you choose when facing life's ups and downs has a powerful impact on the development of your character and courage, as well as your self-image and self-esteem. Why not choose the best version of yourself and live out that story?

Through my coaching programs, my clients learn invaluable skills and undergo a great deal of training that helps them not only face challenges head on, but acquire a toolkit to effectively:

Mindset and Meaning

- navigate their future

- overcome resistance

- improve their ability to creatively solve problems

- discover their courage and character

- obtain a job they love that's also profitable

- ask for a pay rise

- take control in situations involving bullying or harassment

- attract a life partner

- ensure a successful and sustainable long-term relationship

- lose those last ten kilos

Your life experiences hinge on your mindset and the meaning you give to any situation you encounter. You either consciously or unwittingly choose your future, so understanding how to set it to growth is fundamental.

 To discover more about how Rebecca can help you *Elevate Your Mindset*, simply visit www.elevatebooks.com/mindset

Cherry Farrow
Your Best Self

Cherry Farrow is a dynamic, transformational speaker, presenter, master coach and businesswoman who teaches people how to master their life and disrupt their perceived limitations by using her powerful mindset-changing tools and cutting-edge personal development strategies to uncover their true self and leave a legacy.

Through Cherry's hypnosis training, she learned about NLP and Time Line Therapy™. That's when everything had shifted. She started seeing massive results in her life and the positive impact of investing in herself and mindset work.

Cherry's passion to help others achieve their potential and acquire personal abundance is powered by a vision of every human having the ability to unlock their potential and step into their greatness.

Cherry Farrow
Your Best Self

What's the best way to help people?

I've been fortunate to have a huge array of clients coming to me for coaching, training and self-development. They range from business owners and employees who want to improve their career satisfaction by increasing opportunities and acquiring or enhancing leadership skills, to those who want to relieve their depression, PTSD, anxiety or OCD, as well as become a better parent. The list is extensive.

I find that the best way to help people is to get them to understand how they're creating their current life circumstances in the first place, so they're able to improve their communication skills and create massive changes in their life. I always tell my clients, "I'm only a guide." The law of polarity states that for anything to exist, there has to be an equal and exact opposite, so therefore the solution is already inside of them.

I can remember one client who'd suffered from depression for nearly twenty years. He came in, threw his book on the table and said, "I don't even know why I'm here. Nobody can fix me." My immediate response was, "That's right. Nobody can fix you." He was taken aback by my reply because he'd gotten used to being told by doctors, psychologists and psychiatrists that they could fix his problem with depression.

My philosophy is that nobody's broken; they're just running strategies that aren't enhancing their life. As proof, after only a few days, this man announced he was cured of depression.

Now, I didn't cure him. All I did was help him get in touch with resources that were already within him. To this day, he's still free from depression and has an unwavering belief that it will never come back.

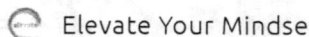 Elevate Your Mindset

That's the power of getting in control of your mind. Whatever you have in your life, both what you do and don't want, is only there because you created it. Now, I'm not saying to blame yourself. What I mean is that you need to look at ways of drawing that line in the sand and moving forward with your life, so you can create what you do want, rather than what you don't.

All it takes is an understanding of who you are and accepting responsibility for your own life. Then you need to take the necessary steps to make those changes happen.

What are the biggest blocks people create to getting what they want?

Over the many years I've spent coaching and training people, I've noticed there are three major issues that hinder them from achieving the success they want in life.

1. **Failing to understand themselves, how they operate and how they filter information**

    In regard to filtering information, every person is made up of different life experiences that are based on memory, life decisions, beliefs adopted over the time, and values, as well as deep, unconscious filters called meta-programmes. These filters are important to understand, especially when you have a goal to accomplish. It will help if you know what language to use to motivate and get the best out of people, whether it's an employee, your children or yourself.

    Meta-programmes, which we teach in our master practitioner trainings, can motivate or de-motivate you. They help filter and process what you experience, which means how you delete, distort and generalise information that comes from the outside world to the point it becomes your reality.

If you have a look at the diagram below, you'll see that an external event is information that's coming from your environment. The only way to process information is through the five senses: what you see, hear, feel, smell and taste. Now, say for example that as a young child you were told you couldn't write well. Then as an adult, whenever you have to write something, you're sure it's going to be awful. So if someone suggests you make even minor changes, you automatically hear them saying you're a horrible writer. What happened is that you only absorbed information that proved you were right. Psychologists call this *confirmation bias*. It's all so you can say, "See? I told you so."

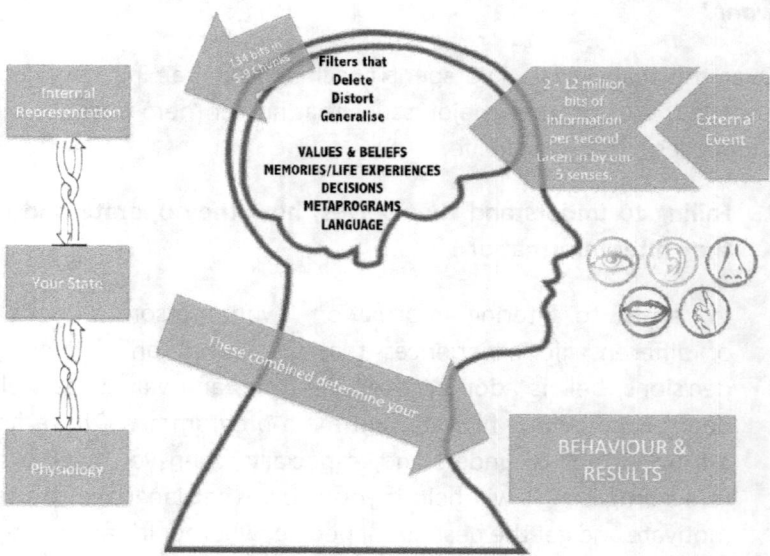

You accept information based on your beliefs, values and life experiences. Someone who had a lot of support and was always encouraged to be successful will filter the information and react differently from a child whose parents always told them, "You'll never amount to anything."

I'd like to clarify what I mean about deleting, distorting and generalising information. Take a few seconds to look around your current environment, wherever you are, and find everything that's red. Then, if you're able to, close your eyes for thirty seconds, and remember everything you saw that was red.

Now, without looking around, try to recall everything that was blue.

You can see how this illustrates what happens when you limit your focus. Unless you were sitting in familiar surroundings, you probably had a hard time remembering any blue objects.

Humans focus on that which they believe is true, and of course, energy flows where attention goes. This creates what's called an *internal representation*, which is what you see, hear, feel and say to yourself. When you distort or delete information, you're more apt to have a negative reaction to certain situations, which keeps producing negative results.

The good news is that once you get a grip on this knowledge, you'll be able to take control of those representations, which will affect your physiology and in turn produce behaviours that create better results. Understanding how you operate will change your misconceptions. I always say it's like getting a grease and oil change.

Once those filters are cleaned, your outlook becomes more life enhancing, which in turn affects your state of mind and physiology to the point your behaviour changes, and you react to situations in ways that produce better results.

2. Believing they have no control over their own lives

In all my years of working with people, I'm constantly told how they're just unlucky, life's dealt them a bad hand and they can't change anything in their life. So it's amazing what happens once they realise they have the power within them to create different neurological pathways and have positive interactions.

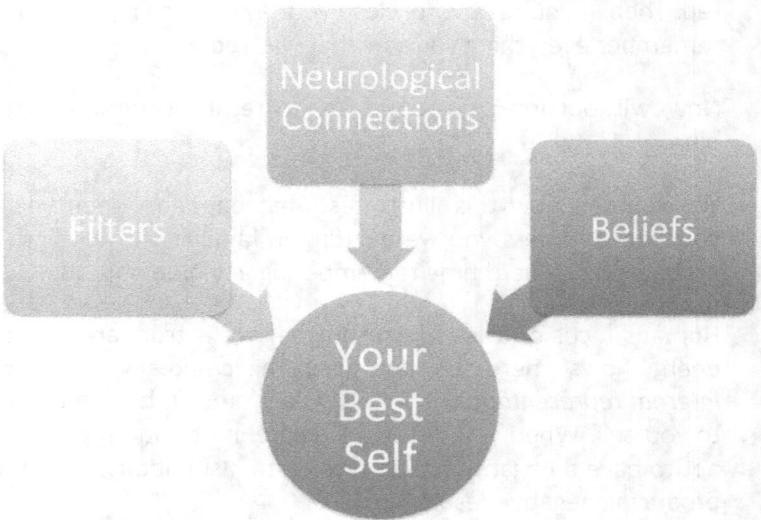

Consider the number of neurological connections you can make as all the grains of sand on all of the beaches in the world or stars in the universe. That's a lot of connections. So imagine how empowered you'll be when you realise that at any given moment, you have trillions and trillions of different ways of assessing a situation or problem. It's up to you to take control and be responsible for your current situation, so you're able to change it.

3. **Holding beliefs that limit them**

Your beliefs limit you. As I said earlier, if you believe you're not good enough, all through your life you're only going to look for ways to prove you're right.

I'm a big fan of twin studies in which two people who grew up in the same house, with the same parents, in the same environment, adopt different beliefs.

One study that stood out for me was a situation where one twin was a highly successful businessman, while the other was an alcoholic who'd given up on life. They asked the successful twin what made him successful, and he said his father was an alcoholic, and he was never going to wind up like that. When they asked the alcoholic twin the same question, he said, "Well, my father was an alcoholic. What do you expect?"

At any time in your life, you have the ability to accept or reject these beliefs. However, most of the time you're not conscious of what you do or don't believe. You're unaware of what your values are or the life experiences that have hindered you, as well as what motivates you and the language you use to communicate what you need. Once you bring this into your consciousness, you'll be able to make the necessary changes to achieve success.

Based on your experience, what's the best tip you could give to someone to help them change their life?

The biggest tip that I could give somebody is to do a Neuro-Linguistic Programming (NLP) training and to make sure it incorporates Time Line Therapy™.

Time Line Therapy was created by Dr. Tad James, and I can say that it's one of the best modalities I've ever come across. I'm one of those people who have a library full of self-help and self-development books. For years I was looking for that one thing that was going to change my life, and when I went and did this NLP training course that incorporated Time Line Therapy, I realised it was what I'd been looking for.

Since then I've become an internationally accredited trainer, and I'm in my fourth year of my Masters program to become a master trainer of NLP, Time Line Therapy, hypnotherapy and an NLP coach. Knowing the effects these techniques and therapies have had on my own life, I felt that continuing with my education was essential, so I could pass this information on to others. I've coached and trained hundreds of people over the years who've all benefitted from these techniques.

Now, while the language model of NLP is amazing, I also believe that Time Line Therapy accelerates your success. It's coaching on steroids.

Whoever you choose for your training, make sure they're accredited, which means they're registered with the Time Line Therapy association. Do your research, because people are starting to realise how effective this therapy is, so there are many who will claim to be trainers or coaches but don't necessarily have the qualifications. Again, it's not something you can learn from a book. You need hands-on experience. Even though I'd read many books about NLP, I never got results until I did face-to-face training.

How can someone develop the best mindset to improve their life?

Invest in yourself. Take trainings that will help you understand why and how you do what you do. For example, at our Release Your Limitations seminar, we talk about goal setting and the triune model of the brain, which are three distinct structures that emerged along an evolutionary path and provide an approximation of the hierarchy of brain functions. By introducing this model, we help people realise their desired goal has to go through three different checkpoints, or roadblocks, before it even has a chance of succeeding.

> **Checkpoint One: The Reptilian Brain (R-Complex)**
>
> Everyone has a reptilian, or primitive brain that's responsible for survival responses, such as fight, flight and freeze. It's the oldest part of the brain.

When you set a goal that's convoluted, your reptilian brain will go into fight or freeze response, because its entire job is to keep you safe. Your goal will get stuck at that checkpoint if the instructions are unclear and seem to interfere with your safety.

▸ **Checkpoint Two: Paleomammalian Complex**

The Paleomammalian Complex is the emotional brain. It will kick in and stop you if you don't get the feelings you need from the goals you're trying to achieve.

▸ **Checkpoint Three: The Neocortex or Neomammalian Complex**

The neocortex, otherwise known as the Neomammalian Complex, is responsible for rationality. If what you're trying to accomplish doesn't seem rational or logical, it won't get through this checkpoint.

We teach in our seminars and trainings how to set goals so you can achieve them consistently, because it takes into account the Triune Brain and the steps every goal has to go through to make sure it meets the requirements of your evolutionary mind. To do what you want in life, you need to know how to make the necessary changes.

What makes people medicate with drugs and other substances, and how do you think medical practitioners and other institutions could be better educated in alternative methods?

I think when people feel they're at the end of their rope and have no other options available, they resort to prescription medication or substance abuse. A lot goes on in the psyche for this to happen.

Of course, all of these medications have a place. I just wish there was a way to spread the news about other possibilities that will help with these conditions. We've worked with people who suffer from depression, anxiety, PTSD, OCD, fibromyalgia, chronic pain, self-harm and bulimia. The list goes on and on of the people we've coached to the point they're living a fulfilling life they love.

Whenever something goes wrong, the first response is to go to a specialist and trust everything they say, because society has programmed people to hand over their lives to medical professionals. When you go to the doctor and they prescribe antidepressants, you just accept that this is the only way to cure your depression and don't question if there are alternative methods.

Doctors are under the pump and don't have time to sit and ask you questions about your life in order to get the big picture of the origins of your issue. People also want a quick fix, so they're more than happy to take a pill for their problems, because they're at their wit's end, and no other viable options are offered. This is where it would be advantageous for us to work together with the medical profession, so people could be referred to practitioners who have time to find out some more history about their patient in order to fully diagnose and treat them.

Inspire & Inform is in the process of introducing this information into schools, so children can learn from an early age how to create their own life. It will help them understand how reality is shaped, so they can adopt a growth mindset and feel empowered.

I just want to get out there and let people know there are many uplifting options that will help them plug into and enjoy their own life, rather than removing themselves from it. The world would be a much better place to live, and people wouldn't have to resort to self-medicating with drugs and alcohol.

In fact, our company has a hundred-percent success rate with helping people achieve their life goals. Those we work with come to realise why they're holding onto their issues, and once they come to this realisation, they have a choice as to whether or not they want to keep going the way they are, or change. In the psychology world we call this *secondary gain*.

But please bear in mind that sometimes this process can be quite frightening. For example, a young man who'd been diagnosed with depression from a young age and had never held down a job, couldn't fathom a life where he wasn't dependent on a disability pension. So what happens is that for someone like him, getting better would seem like a negative, as he wouldn't know what to do with his life once he got better.

I think the conversation needs to start with the best way for people to be rewarded for getting better, but also how to provide assistance until they receive the proper training and get back on their feet. It's a complicated issue. I don't believe people would always choose to take drugs or medication if they knew there was a better and healthier alternative.

A combination of circumstances will make this happen. We need to start getting the word out there by speaking louder and stronger that there are other ways. Inspire & Inform is making inroads in their attempts to offer these trainings to universities and medical practices, so people who are suffering can be made aware of alternative methods to alleviate it.

Why is mindset important?

If you start off with the mindset that you're going to fail at your endeavour, what do you think is your chance of success? Mindset is more than just positive thoughts or affirmations. You're an amazing being with unlimited potential, but you've probably been told throughout your life that your desired goal is impossible and that you don't have the skills, knowledge or stamina to pull it off. If this is coming from a parent or loved one, the message can be powerful enough to stop you before you start.

You need to put yourself in a position to just believe you're capable of getting rid of that self-doubt and critical voice that used to come from outside forces but are now part of your subconscious. Learn how to be your own best friend and tell yourself how great you are and that you can achieve anything. The only way to do that is to have an empowering, limitless mindset that lifts you up.

Inspire & Inform helps people design their life the way they want it. Having the mindset that you're capable of anything is the main ingredient for your success, whether it's in your business or personal life. If you have the right mindset, you can enjoy all you do, get fabulous results and display amazing behaviours.

What is the one message you wish to share with the world?

The one message I would like to share with the world is that everyone has the potential within them to overcome any obstacle. You have an inner wisdom or genius to overcome your problems. All you need are the right tools and the know-how to use them.

What stops you from overcoming these roadblocks are the beliefs you've formed over the course of your life, whether from parents, your social environments or authority figures.

When experiencing any struggles, ask yourself:

- *How is this a struggle?*
- *What are the beliefs behind it, and are they true?*
- *Is what I'm doing enhancing my life, or is it limiting me, and am I ready to let it go?*

You always have a choice, even though right now it may not feel like it. At any time, you can take a different path by resetting or recalibrating your beliefs.

What are you passionate about?

That's an interesting question. I'm passionate about many things, but the major one is to help people step into their greatness by understanding what drives them, and that they have the power within themselves to break through their self-imposed limitations and reach their goals to live a life they love.

What made you choose to specialise in NLP and Time Line Therapy?

I was born in Croatia and moved to Australia at a very young age. When I started school, I couldn't speak a word of English, but I soon developed powerful communication skills and a passion to learn.

After the sacrifices my parents made to bring their family to "The Lucky Country", the ethos was to work hard. There was no talk about going to college or university, or even finishing high school. The focus was on getting a job and paying your way.

Due to the cultural differences and expectations of being the only daughter out of five children, I left home at seventeen and moved to another state. Being young and alone in an unfamiliar environment brought about other challenges, but I retained the mindset that I was a survivor.

I worked hard and rose up through the ranks in any job I had. I got married young, had children young and was doing great in my career, but I still felt something was amiss.

Then when my relationship began faltering, I became an emotional wreck. I knew I had to do something, so I invested in all sorts of self-help books and programs that would bring about results for a short while. But I knew there had to be more.

Eventually I went to a hypnosis training, where I learned about NLP and Time Line Therapy. I became obsessed, because everything started to shift, and I saw massive positive results in my life.

I then committed to learning everything I could within this realm and invested heavily in my self-discovery. Now I help people take control of their own life by teaching them how to master their mindset with my powerful mindset-changing tools and cutting-edge personal development strategies.

What stops someone achieving the success they really want?

First and foremost, it's their beliefs surrounding their ability to achieve success. I think if they do a training, or even hire a coach that's accredited in Time Line Therapy, they'll be able to remove those blockages and realise what's been holding them back, so they can achieve success.

It's possible for anyone to change, but it can't be forced upon them. They have to want it.

What's the best success tip you could ever give?

Invest in yourself. Cut out all excuses and just invest the time, money and effort it takes to design your life the way you want.

How do your trainings and seminars make a difference in people's lives?

I launched Inspire & Inform in 2011 in the hope of inspiring people to take control and become responsible for the direction of their life. I wanted to accumulate all of the training and self-development I'd done over the years and make a comprehensive plan that would show the way for people to live a life they love.

Currently, I run a number of training programmes. There's a seven-day Accelerate Your Success practitioner programme, as well as a fifteen-day Master Your Success programme. I also run a multitude of different seminars and workshops. A popular one is Release Your Limitations, which teaches people about what we call in the NLP world, *cause and effect*. It's about living above the line or below the line; being a victim or a victor. We teach people how to take responsibility for where they are in life and what they can do to change it, so they can achieve success in their endeavours.

I love this quote: "Between stimulus and response lies a space. In that space is our power to choose a response. In our response lies our growth and our happiness." (Unknown)

What this means is that when something happens, you have a space of time, even if it's just a millisecond, to make a decision as to how to respond.

You've probably heard the phrase, "They really pushed my buttons!" Most people have a hot button surrounding certain subjects or situations that makes them explode in anger. According to Victor Frankl, even if you have just a short amount of time to respond, you can choose to react in a different way. This becomes possible once you accept a hundred percent responsibility for everything you do.

In my seminar, I have a fun little exercise where I ask people to partner up and find each other's button.

Of course, once the exercise is complete, people realise those buttons are an internal job, and they're the only ones pushing them. When this happens, it's amazing what a change it makes. They realise they aren't being encouraged by anyone to react the way they do, and they can choose a different response to any situation.

The reality is that no one makes you do anything. You choose to get angry. You choose to get sad. I know it's a hard pill to swallow, but once you're ready to accept that responsibility, it's amazing what a difference it will make in your life.

In our training, we go through the NLP Communication Model, which describes how people filter information received from the external world. Once you understand this, you can make adjustments.

Whatever happens in life, you have to delete, distort and generalise, because your conscious mind can't handle the multitude of information you're bombarded with. It has to chunk it down. Problems only arise when you're deleting, distorting and generalising the wrong information.

In our seminars and workshops, we teach people how to change those filters in a way that will help them, rather than limit them.

We also talk about how people believe they're travelling only one pathway in life, but in reality, there are multitudes they can choose to take. Most people run on autopilot until they start becoming aware of what's holding them back from leading the life they want.

Awareness leads to making the necessary changes. You don't have to run on autopilot. You can consciously control what you do. You're a powerful being.

In our seminars and trainings, we help you release negative emotions. You're able to go through and remove your limiting beliefs, so you can achieve what you want in life, consistently. It's like personal training for the mind, so you can achieve your best results.

Throughout your life, you use your memories to create reference points that dictate how you react in a given situation. If you can imagine removing the negative emotions associated with those events, you'll no longer have them as reference points, and you can start afresh. It makes a massive difference when you can start from a clean slate.

You'll learn about why you achieve some goals, while falling short on others. The best takeaway from these seminars is the ability to set outcomes, so you know without a doubt you can reach them consistently.

For me, there's nothing better than seeing the change in people's faces. Take a look at the photo below. This is Carmen. She did a seven-day Accelerate Your Success training course. The photo on the left was taken on day one, and the one on the right is day seven. She took both photos. Can you see how much more relaxed she looks in the picture on the right? It's almost like getting a facelift. The difference is obvious, and it's just because she released negative emotions and limiting decisions.

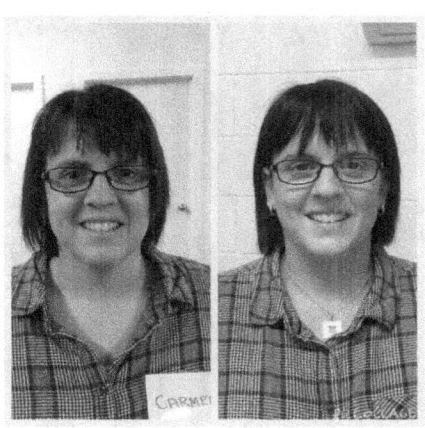

This is why I do what I do. It just warms the cockles of my heart to see the transformations happening right before my very eyes when people have their *aha* moments, followed by the desire to learn and do more. I'm a firm believer that you can always better yourself. You can always expand and grow. I hope to keep it up for many more years to come.

Why should someone work on their mindset?

I think people should work on their mindset if they want to achieve better results in their life and have a desire to control their emotions and emotional intelligence.

By having a growth mindset, you can transform into the person you've always wanted to be. Once you accept that you have the power to dictate your life, you can achieve anything you set your mind to.

How can people become their own success story?

By becoming aware of why they do what they do and how they create what they have in their life, and then taking the steps to change course, so they're heading in the direction they want it to go.

If you'd like more information on our programs, go to www.inspireandinform.com.au

 To discover more about how Cherry can help you *Elevate Your Mindset*, simply visit www.elevatebooks.com/mindset

Sharon Laing PhD

Know Thyself

Sharon Laing is a life coach who combines a background in science, nursing, midwifery, psychology and psychotherapy to inform her work. She's taught, supervised and mentored students across a range of disciplines and settings, and has volunteered in the welfare sector in management, supervision and counselling.

Sharon holds a PhD in Psychology, has published in academic journals and has presented at international conferences.

Through her consultancy business, she provides research, psychological and coaching services to individuals and organisations. Due to her own journey of personal and professional discovery spanning over forty years, she's passionate about personal development and is most inspired by assisting others to grow more confident in their abilities, embrace their personal power, improve their health and lead a more fulfilling life.

Sharon Laing PhD
Know Thyself

How did you become interested in coaching?

I've always been a keen observer of others and what's going on around me. As a naturally curious person, I constantly sought to understand what makes people tick and how the natural world works. So after completing school, I went on to study science at university, which provided the foundations for all of the learning that followed.

At the age of twenty-three, I had an 'aha' experience that led me away from working in laboratories and into hospital-based training to become a registered nurse and midwife. This allowed me to learn about the human body in sickness and health, as well as the miracle of new life and birth.

I became curious about the care of critically ill babies, so I trained and worked for many years in newborn intensive care. From observing people's reactions in various settings and situations, in crisis, triumph and tragedy, I grew curious about the human mind, as well as human behaviour, both individually and within society.

To figure it all out, I returned to university as a part-time student to study psychology and anthropology, before eventually graduating with a PhD in psychology and becoming a therapist, counsellor, teacher of psychology and researcher. I've also explored different spiritual practices throughout the years, all of which deepened my belief that the mind, body and spirit functions as a whole, not as separate entities. Life has also presented me with many of my own personal challenges, losses and lessons that taught me about myself and the concept of compassion.

I've experienced feelings of despair, loneliness, rejection, fear, rage, desolating grief and numbing emptiness in my sixty-three years of life, but people can experience similar events and have totally different reactions. I believe it's presumptuous to say that I know how someone else *must* be feeling. There's no one-size-fits-all rule book. When working with clients, I make a point to not overlay another's personal story with my own. Having similar past experiences doesn't guarantee being able to help someone else deal with it. A wise nurse told me, "You don't need to have had a broken leg to know how to mend one."

Coaching was a natural progression from all that came before. It provided another way of using what I've learnt, both personally and professionally, to focus on helping others believe in their own power and develop strategies to achieve what's meaningful for them. I've been blessed with many wonderful teachers, mentors and supportive people in my life, so I fully appreciate the gift of having someone at your side who holds your best interests at heart and has the skills to guide you. I got into coaching to help others on their journey towards fulfilment and to share in that amazing experience of people embracing their power and living their passions.

If you were speaking to your younger self, what advice would you give?

Believe in yourself. Forgive yourself if you can't live up to your ideal. Always remember that you're a work in progress.

Keep in mind that experiences shape your character. Even when it seems you've gone down a side-track, it will be okay. Perhaps it's a path you're meant to take. You have inside you the power to overcome challenges and disappointments. While it may take longer than you'd like, wounds heal, and your battle scars will serve as reminders of what you've overcome and the lessons you've learned.

It's okay to be afraid and uncertain, or to hesitate at certain times and be impulsive at others. Embrace it all, and don't judge yourself or take on others' judgements. You might make choices that people don't agree with or understand, but it's what you do next that speaks to who you are and who you're becoming.

Take every opportunity to learn about yourself; who and what matters to you, your likes and dislikes and your strengths and abilities. Seek teachers and mentors who show compassion, wisdom and vision, and who believe in you. Listen to others' opinions and judgements with an open mind, but don't accept what they say as gospel truth. Be curious and spend time in reflection, passing their ideas through your filters. Listen to your instincts. The more you follow your intuition, the clearer those messages will become, and the more you'll trust yourself.

Take the initiative. There'll be many people and situations you can't control, but there'll also be many more that will be in your power to influence. Step up to play a leading role in your own life. There will be suffering and sadness, losses and heartache; but you'll also experience incredible joy, love and healing. So buckle up, and enjoy the ride!

What do you think is your life purpose?

It's taken me a long time to realise what I now recognise as my life purpose. I think it was when I took the time to reflect on questions like "Why do I get out of bed?" and "What lights me up?", that my purpose became clearer to me. I feel my life purpose is to help people better understand themselves and claim their power for making life more fulfilling and meaningful.

The way this has played out during my lifetime has changed, but it seems to me that I've always found myself in situations, both private and professional, where I've fulfilled this purpose. Even when I hadn't been aware of what drew me to it. My desire to be of service to others was inspired by my wonderful parents who both showed incredible generosity, a love of learning and a genuine willingness to help others.

Know Thyself

I believe we all have gifts to bring to the world and lessons to learn. Because people can react differently to the same experience, I'm careful not to make assumptions about others based on my own personal story. From a young age, I've learnt to respect the rights of others in determining their own path. Serving them includes honouring their autonomy.

I love teaching in any form, but the biggest 'buzz' for me is witnessing those moments when a client recognises that they have the ability to move forward through their own efforts. I think an effective coach, like a good teacher, acts as an 'awakener'.

My purpose as a coach is to help clients engage with their beliefs about their personal power, their connections with self and others, and finding the right strategies for them to flourish in life.

What do you think are some of the common issues and barriers that hold people back from flourishing in their life?

People can have issues in all areas of life, such as health, wellbeing, relationships, work, career, parenting, or spirituality. These problems can have flow-on effects, leading to problems with addiction, anger, depression, anxiety and other physical and emotional issues. For the most part, a person's age can also influence what they see as their biggest problem at any particular time. Culture, place and time can play a role in what they perceive as their biggest problems, but I think that our shared humanity means some problems are universal.

However, underlying these issues is that people don't know how to embrace change and realise how powerful they really are. Awareness of these issues, and how to work with them, generally isn't taught in school or by their family.

How would you help people with these issues?

I believe the best way I can help is to respect their right to choose their own agenda and support them with my knowledge, experience and skills. Moving beyond problems calls for looking within and transforming vision into action. I think personal transformation must begin with self-awareness, and I firmly believe in the saying '*Know thyself*'.

For many, this is a challenging process. Developing self-awareness demands considerable effort, but the reward is life-changing.

Through my own experiences in personal development, I know it requires a willingness to be open and honest. Seeing yourself as a victim, or 'less than', are ways you give away your personal power and lock yourself into roles that separate you from living a more fulfilling, meaningful life.

Self-awareness is the first step on the path. This knowledge must be put into action. Just remember that being true to yourself isn't an excuse to ignore the needs and rights of others. Rather, it means taking back responsibility for living with integrity and being mindful of not letting others define you or your choices.

The most common barriers to achieving goals are a lack of confidence, practice and structure. People will often blame their genes. For instance, they'll say they aren't talented enough to play piano or they're just naturally stupid at maths/hopeless with technology.

Some people blame others for their problems. Or they'll blame the universe and think it's just the way the world works. Underlying these excuses is a lack of belief in their own power. Overcoming these obstacles starts with an honest and thorough exploration of their mindset.

What is the approach you use in your coaching?

I approach coaching as a process of personal transformation, which isn't about *changing* who you are, but about embracing more of who you *truly* are. Through coaching, I offer clients strategies that help make it possible to live with authenticity and integrity.

My belief is that a client comes to coaching for reassurance, not rescuing. They're not 'broken'. More often, they're simply feeling stuck or overwhelmed.

A coach isn't there to fix you but to help you find your own way towards positive change. It's important to keep in mind that your current behaviours and techniques have gotten you this far, so you obviously possess good survival strategies. It's likely you have strengths you haven't recognised. Or it could be that you're not seeing all you have to offer.

It's possible to adapt qualities you already have to better achieve the life you want. There may be signposts you aren't seeing, can't decipher or may be unwilling to follow until you've let go of the baggage you've been carrying. The important thing is to realise you have resources at your disposal. A skilful coach encourages you to explore your mind, find your own solutions and develop what you need to put these into practice. But it's also important that you take responsibility. If you want things to change, you need to be willing to change.

I firmly believe in a holistic approach to transformation. There's now scientific evidence underpinning vibrational and energetic medicine, the vital interplay of environment and genetics, and the power of the mind. I think that whatever resonates within you as an individual has a role to play in regard to your personal journey towards happiness, wellbeing and fulfilment. As a coach, I know there are times when a client might benefit from the services of someone with skills in areas other than my own, and this becomes part of the process.

Over the years, I've come to believe there are three important aspects to helping people change their outlook and improve their lives, and I incorporate them into my coaching. They are the 3-M's:

▶ **Mindset**

- Go from a fixed to a growth mindset
- Practice to achieve Mastery
- Develop your 'mental muscle' for facing challenges

▶ **Motivation**

- Maintain the momentum of change
- Make changes that are meaningful for you
- Take action to start movement towards goals

▶ **Methods**

- Be time sensitive, not controlled by time
- Tailor-fit strategies by tracking your progress
- Learn techniques for your personal tool-kit

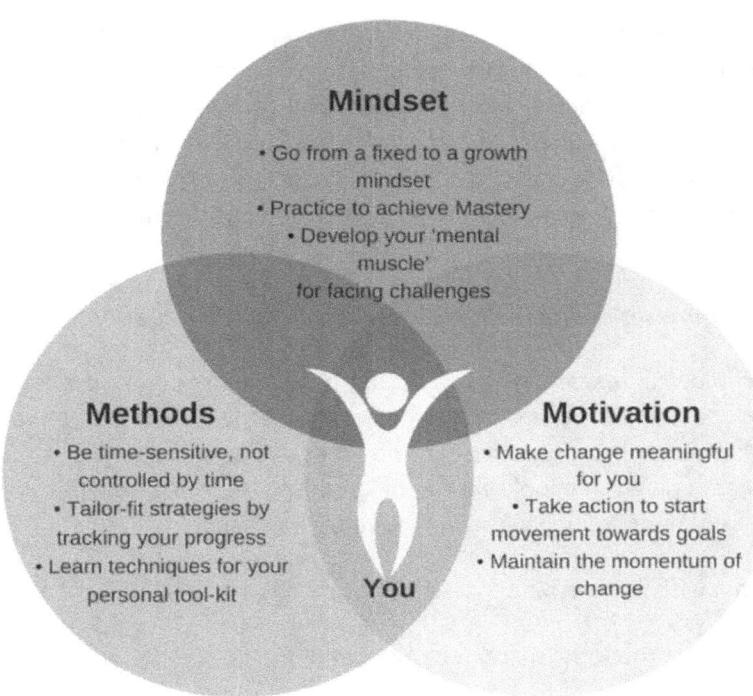

Figure 1. The 3-M Model of Transformational Change

As Figure 1 illustrates, each of these aspects informs the others. Their interwoven nature guides my coaching.

What does the term mindset mean to you, and why is it important?

To me, the term mindset means the way you view your life and experiences, and the meaning you give to them. It's an attitude and outlook you use to navigate your way through life. Mindset colours how you see yourself, others and the world. Essentially, it's the lens through which you view everything going on around you and the person looking back at you from the mirror. It's important, because it influences your beliefs about your chances of success and the actions you take towards living your dreams.

Mostly though, people aren't aware they're looking at people and situations through their own personal set of lenses and just how much they may be distorting what they see, not just on the outside but on the inside as well. I believe that mindset is crucial to the success of coaching, because it basically defines a person's attitude in regard to the challenges they face and the effort they put into achieving what they want.

What mindset do you believe is needed to create a great life?

Psychological research shows that a growth mindset, as opposed to a fixed mindset, is a prerequisite for personal growth. Because mindset determines what you strive for and what you see as success, a mind that's set on growth looks for opportunities to learn and develop, while the fixed mindset believes they're unable to change.

People with a growth mindset:

- believe that qualities can be nurtured

- take responsibility for their success and put in the necessary effort

- prioritise learning over results and welcome the chance to grow

- see learning as fun and failure as feedback that provides an opportunity to improve

- believe that life's setbacks can be converted into future successes through effort and learning

- see others' success as a source of encouragement and seek out such people as mentors and teachers

In contrast, people with a fixed mindset:

- believe that a person's abilities are set in stone and are constantly seeking validation

- believe that if you're already gifted, talented, or brilliant, you don't need to make any effort

- blame other factors rather than acknowledge a lack of skills that could be improved with effort

- would rather not try than fail, because failure and mistakes erode their self-belief

- don't want anyone to see them struggling, so they don't ask for help

- feel threatened by the success of others and are supersensitive to negative feedback

- restrict their ability to fulfil their potential

What's the best way for someone to develop a growth mindset?

Essentially, reorienting your mindset involves rewiring your brain, which takes courage and flexibility. One important aspect of cultivating a growth mindset is to acknowledge that your genes are not the ultimate determinant of your fate. Instead, environmental factors establish which genes are 'activated'. This means, for example, you may not be doomed to pessimism; that by learning and doing whatever it takes to turn these feelings around, it's possible to activate your 'optimistic' genes.

Language is powerful and can help or hinder your growth and success, so start by reframing it. Studies show that people are influenced by thoughts they're not even consciously aware of. Examine the language you habitually use. This includes your internal dialogue, because it determines the filters through which you see yourself, others and the world.

Over time, you can create negative beliefs that limit how you think about opportunities, choices and growth, which often results in self-fulfilling prophecies. A different interpretation of a situation can give you more choice over your reactions. For instance, mistakes become lessons, and endings become new beginnings.

Learning to be more comfortable with change can start with using the language of possibilities and challenging negative beliefs. For example, it's helpful when you're learning a new skill to reword, "I can't do that" with "I can't do that *yet*." You have to believe that change is possible and that thinking this way can actually make a difference.

Everybody is resistant to changing their perspective and sometimes don't even realise they're distorting their perceptions. However, there are techniques you can learn for adjusting your world outlook and reorienting your mindset.

Why should someone work on their mindset?

Your mindset isn't constant. It can vary over time and in different situations, so it's not a case of *set and forget*. Anyone can have fixed mindset moments when they're so busy mentally judging or emotionally reacting, that they don't see the opportunities for learning and improvement.

Being open to new ways of looking at situations is a challenge, because you aren't always aware when you're doing it. This means it's important to tune into your attitudes and reactions, especially when the 'going gets tough'. In those instances, it might be time for a mind reset.

According to well-renowned psychologist Carol Dweck, the first step towards changing your mindset is to understand how your brain works. Imaging has shown the brain's ability for neuroplasticity; that is, in response to your thoughts and actions, the brain creates new neural pathways and keeps wrapping these in myelin to speed up how quickly they conduct messages. Repeated practice creates faster, more efficient pathways, which leads to mastery. People with a growth mindset understand that the human brain has the ability to support lifelong learning.

Neuroimaging proves that your brain responds to use in the same way a muscle does, which means the more you use it, the stronger it becomes. And if you don't use it (or abuse it), you lose it. History has taught us that it's not the strongest species that survives, it's the most adaptable one, and adaptability relies on 'mental muscle'. When you use feedback and alter your strategies accordingly, you're exercising your mental muscle and using it to overcome the common barriers in life, such as a lack of confidence, practice and structure.

True self-confidence is reflected in your mindset. It's the courage to stay open to change and be willing to grow, even when you feel vulnerable. Confidence can be nurtured to a healthy level using three key principles:

1. Leaving your comfort zone.

2. Rewiring your brain instead of ruminating.

3. Embracing 'fast-failure'.

Hanging out in your comfort zone can mean getting trapped into doing what you've always done, because it feels familiar and safe. But nothing new happens if you stay there.

Regularly pushing yourself outside of your comfort zone gives you the courage to take risks. There are several simple, yet effective ways of ensuring a successful outcome, including:

- thinking less
- acting more
- starting small

There are also several effective techniques to stop ruminating, which is the process of putting your thoughts on a loop and changing the track that's playing in your head. These techniques will rewire your brain with new neural pathways. Some of the techniques that help rewire your brain include:

- becoming aware of, and changing, automatic negative thoughts
- doing meditation
- cultivating an attitude of gratitude

Whenever you learn something new, you become conscious of your incompetence. At this point, you have the choice to give up or keep going. The resiliency it takes to withstand setbacks and remain confident when confronting difficulties can be learnt.

'Fast-failure' is a technology buzz-word that refers to releasing a product quickly to test it in the marketplace and then making adjustments based on feedback. Often the world won't wait for perfection. Experiencing 'fast-failure' can build resiliency and confidence. Accepting feedback that something isn't 'perfect' and being willing to make adjustments as needed, reinforces a growth mindset, because it reminds you that you have the ability to learn and develop.

A lack of practice translates to a lack of opportunities for exercising your mental muscle and rewiring your brain. Getting into an 'as if' mindset is all about focusing on a positive mental state and acting as if you're already the person you want to be. There's evidence that the physical act of smiling can cause the brain to produce the neurochemicals that make you feel happy, which can change your way of thinking and feeling.

A lack of structure leaves too much space for distractions, interruptions and procrastination. Having systems in place, such as routines and rituals, can help streamline your time, so your efforts are more productive. A good way to increase efficiency is working to a structure rather than your moods.

How does someone stay motivated in achieving their goals?

It's not uncommon for people to start out on a journey of change, only to let their efforts fall by the wayside. Knowing what motivates you to get on track and stay there is self-awareness in action. Meaning, movement and momentum play a crucial role in motivation.

▸ **Meaning**

Your emotional brain needs to be engaged to get motivated and learn, so it looks for patterns to create meaning. What you regularly think is what you end up believing, and your values develop from your beliefs. Changing your thinking can create new meanings that will help you achieve desired outcomes. Every person has ideals or concepts they most value and are important in spurring them to take action. Whether you're aware of these values consciously or unconsciously, it makes little difference as to how strongly they drive you in your behaviours and choices.

While most people are willing to name values that seem noble and honourable, such as generosity, perseverance and kindness, there are also feelings you seek out that you might not be so willing to speak of. These are sometimes referred to as shadow values, and they include feelings of superiority, authority, power and control.

Owning your shadow values, and learning how to meet them in healthier ways, allows you to exercise conscious choice in your behaviours. There are many excellent tools for identifying your values. Believing that change can happen, and that *you* can make it happen, is vital to your motivation. When your actions are in synchrony with your values, you feel invested in, and committed to, making changes.

▶ **Movement**

As Benjamin Harvey says, "Life rewards action". You have to do more than *think* differently, you have to *behave* differently and deliberately. Just staying in motion along your path can keep you on track and progressing. It also provides a sense of control. Baby steps are fine. It's not intensity but consistency that matters. Everyday actions, and how steadily you keep applying yourself to practicing those actions, will get you where you want to go.

Concentrate on your strengths, and hone your strong points. Accept that change takes effort and deliberate practice, and show yourself the same compassion you offer others.

It's hard to challenge limiting beliefs and habitual reactions, in part because you use these as excuses for your behaviours. Performing a new action can rewire new neural pathways in an instant, but habits and comfort zones are formed by repetition. New habits and skills also require practice. Each successful action motivates you to continue, but you have to make a start.

▸ **Momentum**

Once you get going, you need to *keep* going. Staying motivated is crucial. A little consistency becomes a lot of motivation. Investing in self has a compounding effect, in that the rewards build on themselves. New experiences can help you to see the world through a fresh perspective, which can open you up to new possibilities you may never have contemplated before.

While staying motivated requires constant attention and effort, it doesn't have to mean putting pressure on yourself. It's about finding what stimulates your continued progress and the tools you need to overcome resistance. Praise yourself for your efforts and progress, and use this to strengthen your resolve. The rate of your progress will depend upon many factors. The important thing is to avoid stagnation. Inspiration feeds momentum.

What are some of the methods people can use to stay inspired on a daily basis?

There are numerous strategies, so it's important to find what works best for you. Inspiration feels like taking a deep breath of fresh air; the invigoration animates you.

It's important to stay connected to whatever you find inspiring. This could include uplifting poetry or literature, stories of people who've overcome adversity to achieve their dreams or listening to music that moves you to thinking beyond your current challenges.

Maybe watching your role models on YouTube or other media can spark your imagination to greater heights. Staying in contact with supportive friends and a network of people you admire will encourage you to pursue your dreams. A supportive environment can amplify your motivation. The key is to do whatever it takes on a *daily* basis. Even if it's a small action or quiet moment for solitude, it will help you stay connected to your inner wellspring of inspiration.

You are your own best healer. You probably know the answers you're searching for but might not be acting on them for a variety of reasons. It reminds me of the story about the man searching for his keys. When a stranger comes to help and asks where he dropped them, the man points to a dark, shadowy area. When the stranger then asks, "So why are you searching over here?" the man replies, "This is where the light is." The lesson here is that sometimes you need to shine light in new directions to find what you're looking for. As a coach, I see my role as helping you to aim your light where it most helps you reconnect with your wisdom. Your success depends in large part on choosing methods that work best for you.

I draw on techniques from an array of helping modalities, from psychology to spiritual practices. Keeping a gratitude diary is a simple technique. Research shows that having an attitude of gratitude increases happiness and optimism and is linked to success. It can remind you to enjoy the little moments rather than spinning out over minor disappointments, disagreements or irritations.

Techniques for change also include:

▸ **Lifestyle choices**

   Some of the elementary aspects of daily life, such as how you refuel, reinvigorate and rest your body, greatly impact your resilience for facing difficulties and making changes. You can drain your energy through a lack of nutritious food, dehydration, and poor lifestyle choices. Healthy lifestyle habits supply the brain with the glucose and oxygen it needs to support optimal function.

▸ **Visualisation**

   Visualisation is a powerful technique for focusing your mind. Neuroscience has demonstrated that your brain doesn't differentiate between what you imagine and what's actually happening. You can change your present behaviour by altering your vision of the future.

Visualisations need to be detailed and deliberately structured, including the sights, sounds, and feelings you want to have. To ensure you're designing a self-fulfilling prophesy of success rather than self-sabotaging, it's important you set up these mental rehearsals so that your brain connects with the outcome you want.

There are many useful self-help books and techniques being promoted in the marketplace. While these work wonderfully well for some, they may not be for everyone. When certain techniques don't work for you, it's easy to feel like a square peg in a round hole and judge yourself negatively. I don't believe in the one-size-fits-all approach. As a coach, I need to remain flexible and be guided by my client's feedback in order to track their progress and tailor techniques to their unique individual needs and preferences.

Most people want to be Time Lords and not Time Slaves. Some of my clients want fast results because they believe their issue comes with a deadline. But releasing the need for immediate results, and being committed to a process rather than a goal, will help them more in the end.

Essentially, your speed of progress will depend on many factors but includes the degree of effort you invest into getting the results you want, as well as how quickly we work together to find the right fit for you. Often it requires courage to take that first step, but the more action you take, the more feedback we'll have available to judge what works most effectively for you.

For instance, you may need time to go away, reflect and imagine. Change is difficult, and the parts of your brain that were designed to keep you safe are always assessing the environment, both inside and out, for anything that threatens the status quo or looks unfamiliar. It's not unusual to discover you're self-sabotaging just at the point when things are changing. It's a natural survival instinct. You want to stay safe, and often *different* can be interpreted by your brain as *dangerous*, so you pull back from the precipice that could launch you into the next phase of your life. It's an unconscious reaction with a highly emotional charge.

Outside of your awareness, you attempt to make logical sense of this by coming up with all sorts of reasons and justifications as to why it's not the right time, or the right change, or the right path for you. But again, some understanding and knowledge, and a greater degree of self-awareness, can help you deal with these moments. Transformation isn't a once-and-for-all thing, but a lifelong journey in which you're constantly learning and changing behaviours that aren't working.

Structuring time is a valuable strategy to add to your personal toolkit. Prioritising, organising your environment, and using systems and routines are strategies that help you focus on practice and work to increase your productivity and enhance performance. It's also important to take time out to do activities you enjoy and to relax, providing it isn't taking you off your path of progress. Daily rituals can help create a sense of freedom through structured time. Remember that you're a free spirit. Don't forget to do something fun, silly or exciting. Be playful and whimsical. Life is too short.

 To discover more about how Sharon can help you *Elevate Your Mindset*, simply visit www.elevatebooks.com/mindset

Elissa Freeman

A Creative Mind

Elissa Freeman is a speaker, trainer and coach who started Business for Creatives to help people profit from their natural talents, whether it's in visual arts, writing or music. She gets them to break through their barriers to confidence and success, and build resilience in the face of adversity.

Elissa's been featured in multiple publications and on various TV shows. She's also an award-winning poet, fashion designer and photographer.

Elissa bridges the gap between creativity and business. She takes cutting-edge communication and professional development skills, runs them through her highly creative brain and presents them in a way that's engaging and makes sense for the creative person.

Elissa Freeman
A Creative Mind

What incidents have impacted you and changed the course of your life?

When I was nine years old, I was sitting on the green lounge in my home in Noosa. I could hear the distant waves crashing on the beach, coupled with the taste of salt in the warm air. Every wall was filled with art, and every surface with sculptures. A piano stood in the corner. This was my home.

Mum told me, in no uncertain terms, to sit on the couch and not interrupt or bother her as she talked to the stranger in the lounge. There she stood, her long, chocolate-brown hair wound up into a bun, wearing a batik dress she'd designed, printed and made herself, thick coke bottle glasses with a black frame, and her most comfortable sandals. She was speaking to a woman with bleached-blonde hair pulled back into a ponytail, decked out in the latest white designer beachwear and dripping in gold jewellery. Mum was stumbling over her words while breathing shallowly, as a bead of sweat formed on her temple.

I didn't understand what was being said, but it was clear to me something was terribly wrong, and I couldn't do anything about it. A knot formed in my stomach.

After some time, the woman left, and mum slumped down on the couch next to me with a deep sigh. "Mum, what's wrong?" I asked anxiously. She locked an intense gaze on me and said, "I just sold a painting."

This event left a long-lasting impression on me that life was difficult for creative people.

After watching my mum struggle, I dedicated myself to helping people overcome whatever stops them from enjoying their creativity. I started Business for Creatives to help creative people understand how to make money from their art, break through any barriers to their confidence and success and build their resilience in the face of adversity.

Mum has since passed away, but I still see part of her in every work of art and creative person I help.

What is the one message you wish to share with the world?

Your creative endeavours are valuable. Boldly step forward to share your art and vulnerability with the world. This is where the base of your power dwells. The world needs your art.

Can you imagine a planet without literature, visual and performance art, music and dance? It would be a very dull place, indeed.

Put aside any thoughts that your work isn't good enough or that people won't enjoy it. I can promise you there will always be those who won't appreciate your creations and be quite vocal about it. But just as you might relate to some art and not others, everyone has the right to their own preference.

It also might surprise you that even the people closest to you can be harsh critics. It doesn't feel pleasant, but you must find the strength within you to keep putting your projects out into the world. There will be those who understand your vision and those who don't. Focus on the ones with whom you connect.

Learn to embrace the critics. They may even do you a favour by bringing attention to your work and will keep you on your toes to always strive to do your best.

When you value your creations, you're valuing your ability to birth them from concepts to their own entity, and set them free in the world to move, inspire, calm, humour and impassion others. Just keep creating.

Do you believe anyone can be creative, even if they couldn't make art?

At some point, people are either told they're creative or they aren't, and they spend their life believing it.

You might think you're not creative, but it's simply not true. Perhaps you don't write, play an instrument or paint, but everyone has an innate sense of creativity. As a creative coach, I work with those inside and outside of The Arts who want to come up with exciting and different solutions to life's challenges, express themselves and reach their desired goals.

If you've ever had an idea, you were being creative. You may have expressed it through:

- Painting
- Drawing
- Playing a song
- Writing
- Figuring out a solution to an engineering or maths problem
- Organising your logistics to deliver the most efficient use of time and energy.

If you have a brain, you're creative.

According to Paul King, Theoretical Neuroscientist, creativity can't be assigned to one part of the brain but is a whole-brain activity. Your creativity expands when your skills, experience, information and perceptive styles from all parts work together. Your brain investigates and arranges many varied paths of thinking and feeling when it's being creative.

Because I deal with the mindset of creatives, I dance between psychology, my business and my own creative endeavours. Understanding the mind and brain, and setting up and running a business, are similar to The Arts, because these areas aren't as different as may have previously been thought.

My family weren't business people or trained in mindset, but being brought up in an arty family certainly helped me hone my eye to see light, shade, colour and balance. It also taught me how to listen to each note and layering of a piece of music, and to appreciate poetry. What I found is that in learning creativity, business and mindset, and applying them, I was lit up in the same way The Arts affect me. They work as a multimedia painting that brings different elements together to form a masterpiece.

What's the biggest tip you can give to creatives launching a business?

The biggest tip I can give is to be persistent. It takes time to move your creations into the business world. Overnight success takes many years before reaching the tipping point. You must be passionate about your art form. It will never work if you're turning your creativity into a business just for the money, which I can promise you is short-lived and unsatisfying.

You must want to be in business because your creativity consumes you, your soul sings when you create and you have a burning desire to share your creations with the world.

I'd advise you not to rush it, but giving yourself time for success doesn't mean sitting around waiting for it to happen or for someone to validate you. It means giving it all you've got and acquiring a good team of people who believe in what you're trying to accomplish.

Your persistence and dedication to your creative business is the essential ingredient to your success. You must have a flexible, yet workable plan, and dogged persistence. You have it in you. I know it. You wouldn't be reading this if you didn't. When I coach a creative person, the concept of persistence is one of my key points.

What I mean about being persistent is to keep doing what you need to do. If it becomes too much and you're not enjoying the process, taking a little time off at intervals is fine, as long as you get back to it.

Also, be resilient to those who tell you to give up what you're trying to accomplish. Like me, you might be told you should just get a job. Be prepared to hear these kinds of things, brush them aside and keep working towards your goals.

Choose to be in the company of people who are supportive yet hold you to a high standard. As much as possible, avoid the company of anyone who puts you down, even in humour, or those who are self-destructive, untrustworthy or don't have your best interest at heart. Of course, this goes both ways; you also need to be a just, fair and loving person to them as well.

I've had to let go of people in my life who didn't support my dream. This is never pleasant, but it can be done with compassion.

Why is it important to create goals?

Goal setting is vital to your success. The evidence is overwhelming. One example is Terence R. Mitchell's article "Motivation: New Directions for Theory, Research, and Practice" published in the *Academy of*

Management Review. Mitchell found goal setting increased motivation so much, that they were completely intertwined.

There are numerous ways to set and plan your goals. In my Artful Aims online program, I teach the top goal-setting systems that work well with the creative mind. There are many techniques in circulation, but only a few of them work. When a person's goals don't come to fruition, it can lead to disappointment and a sense of failure and lowered self-esteem. Often the person isn't the problem; it's the process that lets them down.

One question I'm frequently asked by my creative clients is how they would know if their goals are too big or too small for the time they've allotted to achieve them. I've come up with three easy steps to make this determination:

1. **Review past goals and if you achieved them**

    If you've rarely reached your goals, they probably need to be broken down into smaller components and worked on one at a time.

    On the other hand, if you easily reach your goals without much effort, it could be that you're not taking enough risks. Figure out how you can make them more challenging but not so difficult you feel overwhelmed.

2. **Manage your time wisely**

    In the past, have you set what you thought was a reasonable time frame to achieve your goals, only to let everything else get in the way, so you missed deadline after deadline?

    Like most people, you may have a family, a job and a social life that prevents you from concentrating on your goal to the exclusion of everything else. When setting a time frame, you must take into account the other areas of your life that require attention.

3. Write down your goals

The Harvard MBA Program did a noteworthy study on their students. They looked at the difference between those who wrote down their goals and those who didn't. Only three percent of the whole group had written goals and had a plan of action, thirteen percent had goals in mind but didn't write them down and eighty-four percent had no goals at all.

After ten years, the same people were interviewed again. While the group who had goals in their head and didn't write them down earned twice as much as the group who had no goals, the group that had written them down earned, on average, ten times more than the other ninety-seven percent combined.

When you see it all laid out, you'll be able to determine whether you're taking on too much or if the goal is too easy and won't achieve what you want it to.

If you're a creatively expressive person, you will be motivated and accomplish more when you write down goals and take them one step at a time. Your goal setting and execution should make sense and not be too easy or too difficult.

If you're finding your emotional or psychological mindset blocks you from getting started or progressing with your goals, you're giving up before you get there, or you're sabotaging and/or allowing others to sabotage your goal journey, you will benefit from receiving mentoring or coaching.

> "Our goals can only be reached through a vehicle of a plan, in which we must fervently believe, and upon which we must vigorously act.
> There is no other route to success."
> ~Pablo Picasso

A Creative Mind

What are some of the common barriers creative people experience?

Having had the privilege of working with hundreds of creative people on a global scale, I've found that many of them make the same mistakes over and over again and wonder why they don't achieve the success they could have.

Below are the five simple actions it takes to achieve success. If you practice them religiously, they will become a natural way of being. You don't need to be a genius or even have an interest in creative activities. You just need to give it a try and not let go.

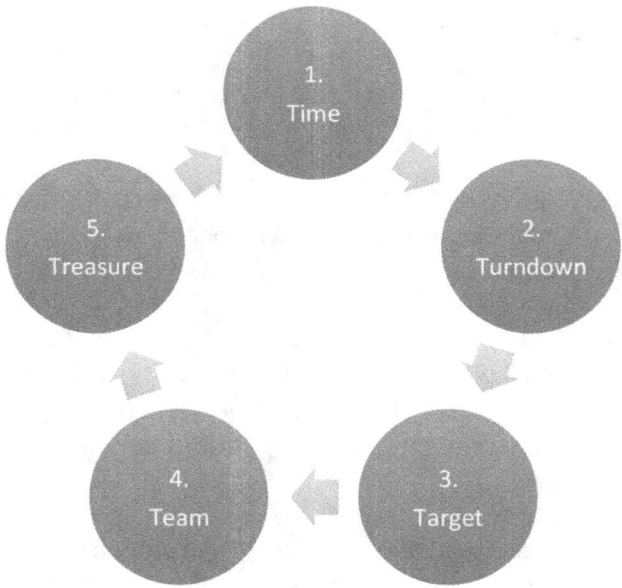

▶ **TIME**

Notice your own energy rhythms, and try to sculpt your day around them. Working from home can be a problem due to friends and family interrupting you. Make them aware of your working hours, so they know not to disturb you during that time.

According to a study done by Dr. De Woot, a leading expert in time management, executives encounter interruptions such as an unexpected visitor, a phone call or a technical glitch every eight minutes, after which it takes them a couple of minutes to regain concentration. Going by this statistic, forty percent of your time is being used up on something other than your most important task. That's an enormous amount of time spent on activities that won't help you achieve your goals.

Set aside time for creating, and don't let anything distract you from it.

▶ **TURNDOWN:**

Do you make commitments without thinking and then feel like you have to follow through?

Practice saying "no", or give yourself time before agreeing to anything, and keep doing it until you become an expert at it. You have every right to refuse a request.

By saying "no" with love, compassion and thoughtfulness, you'll feel more comfortable that your friends and family understand exactly where you stand. Just know they'd be saddened if they thought honouring a commitment to them meant you'd be compromising your business.

A study on refusal motives, conducted and published in the *Journal of Consumer Research,* states there's a difference between saying, "I can't" and "I don't." "I can't" is a reminder of your limitations. "I don't" implies you're empowered and have drawn a line in the sand.

> "People think focus means saying "yes" to the thing you've got to focus on. But that's not what it means at all. It means saying "no" to the hundred other good ideas that there are. You have to pick carefully. I'm actually as proud of the things we haven't done as the things I have done. Innovation is saying no to a thousand things."
> ~Steve Jobs

▸ TARGETS

How many targets do you have at one time?

If you've ever watched *Shark Tank*, you'll notice that none of the panel ever invests if the owner has another business or a secure fulltime job. They mention numerous times that this split focus would be destructive to the success of a business, because the owner wouldn't be able to give their full energy to more than one target at a time.

When ideas come to you, write them down in as much detail as possible, so your brain will calm down and allow you to concentrate on your current target. Then when you've completed your project, you can refer to your list and choose another. Using this method will increase your focus and clarity.

If you focus on more than one target, your commitment weakens, so you can become scattered and have numerous unfinished projects. Put your eye on the target, and don't take it off unless you're willing to let it go for good.

It's better to only have one main creative outlet until you're successful, while keeping the others as a hobby. Once you've set up your business and have systems in place for it to run passively, or mostly passively, you can then choose another outlet on which to focus.

▸ TEAM

Without an effective team, your creative outlet and projects will take longer to accomplish and drain your energy.

A good question to ask yourself is, *Am I the only person who can do this job?* If someone else can do it, then you should delegate it, but always make sure it's the right person.

A study published in the *Harvard Business Review* in 2016 found that delegation increased the delegator's income from twenty to fifty percent and that if you're swamped and need to turn down work, you're not delegating enough.

As your expertise increases, you will need a team that can grow their own expertise, or you need to upgrade your team. With a good easy-to-follow written system, your team will know exactly what's expected of them.

▸ TREASURE

Do you treasure yourself?

It's important you not only understand that you are your greatest treasure, you need to fully embody it.

Everyone is born perfect, divine and worthy. A genuine treasure. Over time, as those you look up to say you're not good enough and are uninteresting, unworthy and lacking in perfection, you can begin to believe the lies.

Being perfect, divine and worthy is your default. And once you begin removing the lies, you'll be left with who you really are—a treasure.

What were some limiting beliefs you had about yourself that held you back?

For much of my life I had significantly poor self-worth, so much so that I didn't feel I had the right to exist. I thought if anyone saw me without heavy makeup, they would be repulsed and sickened by my appearance. I believed I was stupid and dumb, and I carried these beliefs around with me constantly. They affected everything I did and were reflected in everything I said.

It has taken much commitment and dedication to find the truth of my value under layers of illusion. I worked with coaches, read empowering books, invested in trainings, stopped watching TV, meditated and kept good company. By changing my mindset, I slowly shed the noxious layers of these illusions and learned to see myself for the treasure I was.

Did you have a big aha moment that changed your perspective?

For me there was no big AHA moment that changed the way I saw myself. It was just a series of many little realisations backed up by small shifts in my lifestyle and day-to-day activities.

An example of this is the mirror technique. For many years, after I brushed my teeth in the morning I would look into my eyes in the mirror and tell myself:

- You are beautiful

- You are worthy

- I love you

- Thank you

The mirror technique is taught in many personal development programs and books, and that's because it works. But you need to commit to the process and stick to it. Many people stop before they get there.

I had a slow progression through the years. At first, I could only say these things when I had a full face of makeup on, while feeling awkward and uncomfortable, and many different emotions surfaced. After a while, I could make the statements without wearing makeup, but it could still be uncomfortable, and at times it was easier than others. I could burst into tears or laugh out loud.

Having a healthy self-image is similar to exercise. It's a muscle that needs to be worked on regularly. For instance, going for one workout won't keep you fit for the rest of your life. This is a regular exercise that gets easier and eventually becomes enjoyable. There's no quick fix. It takes time and effort to remember the truth of who you are.

Whenever my self-worth takes a dip, I go back to this process. In the beginning I did it every day. Now I use it as a top up when required and will probably use it regularly for the rest of my life. It's as important as sleep, hydration, and sustenance.

What part does meditation play in gaining clarity?

I've been meditating since I was nine. I don't know how I would have gotten through my trials of life without meditation. It keeps me balanced and centred.

When I'm meditating, I get clarity on what's troubling me, and it calms me.

I use many different techniques and meditate from five to thirty minutes in a session. The ones I often return to are where I focus on my breath, ask a question of my unconscious and feel what pops up.

Another is going step by step through my body, relaxing each part.

Most mornings I meditate before I get up and start my day. If something is troubling me, I may meditate for a few minutes before I go to sleep at night as well. Meditation keeps me stable.

What effect does the media have on a person's mindset?

Television can be informative and entertaining. However, many ads and shows send the message that you're not enough, and they have the magic ingredient that will make you worthy, such as a new car, exercise machine, diet food or makeup.

Choose what you watch carefully, and make sure there are no ads. Try to select only entertainment that makes you laugh, feel inspired and happy or educates you. Rather than watching the news, stay informed by perusing the headlines and reading helpful articles. It's also good to avoid viewing anything that makes you fearful or lose faith in humanity.

How can a mindset coach help you achieve your goals?

Working with good mindset coaches can help you see things in yourself you might miss and encourages you to be accountable. Receiving coaching can be essential for building your self-worth and getting to personal and professional goals. It's great to have someone in your corner.

A good coach has always been an important member of my team. I don't believe we're meant to overcome our challenges all alone.

How can someone stay inspired on a daily basis?

Some good ways to stay inspired are limiting TV watching, allocating time to daydream, exercising and spending as much time as possible in nature. It's also good to surround yourself with beautiful art, music and poetry.

But even on those days when you have trouble feeling inspired, don't let it stop you.

Stay motivated by setting your own deadlines and rewards, because you can't always rely on other people to supply them for you. Make sure you have a good motivator to turn up and honour your commitment, such as scheduled meetings and events.

If you know where inspiration comes from, it's easier to access it. Inspiration doesn't originate from outside of you, even though it may seem that way. If you're alive, you can be inspired. It's separate from feelings of happiness or sadness and comes from deep within you. It's your life force.

Have you ever watched an inspirational talk and felt inspired? It wasn't the talk. Whatever the speaker said resonated within you, and you connected with it to the point that it allowed your own inspiration to bubble to the surface.

These three steps can help you manage your external circumstances and be able to create, even if your emotions are affecting your thoughts.

1. Question what you watch, listen to and read.

Ask yourself if what you're watching, listening to or reading is inspiring you. If not, refocus your energies on something that will. It may take some practice, as it means replacing old habits you may have had your whole life.

Over the years, I've accumulated a vault of inspirational articles, movies and clip recommendations that I send my creative clients to trigger their inspiration.

2. **Work on your creative projects every day.**

    Pick up your creative tools and get to work. Even if it's just dabbling, do something toward your goals every day. Roald Dahl, the prolific author, wrote every day from 10.30am to 12pm, had lunch, and then wrote from 4pm to 6pm. He was strict with his routine, because writing was important to him.

    If he was in the middle of a story and lost his inspiration, he'd pull out a clean sheet of paper and write any words or phrases that came to mind, or would use this time to write nonsense and make up words. If you read his books or watch any of the movies based on them, you will notice strange, funny and quirky made-up words. A number of these little diversions became complete books in their own right.

    Roald Dahl refused to be limited by what was going on around him or his emotions. Because of this, he left a legacy that continues to delight audiences all over the globe.

3. **Take a good look at the people with whom you choose to surround yourself.**

    The people you spend time with have a significant influence on your patterns of thought, habits and attitude.

    When you're with someone, ask yourself these questions:

    - Do I you feel uncomfortable or used?

    - Am I being talked into doing things that make me feel less then calm, centred or aware?

    - Is this person trying to coerce me into only thinking their way?

    - Do I fear them or walk on eggshells around certain subjects?

    - Am I unable to be myself?

If you answered yes to any of these questions, you might want to look at removing these people from your life.

The company you keep includes your friends, family, housemates and work colleagues. If you're unable to extract yourself from the company of those who aren't the best for you, limit your time with them. You don't have to be cruel about it or start an argument with them. I'm a strong advocate of loving these people from afar.

Over a thirty-year period, Dr. David McCelland of Harvard University did research on a group of people and who they habitually chose to associate with, and found that it determined an enormous ninety-five percent of their success or failure in life.

Think about the person you spend the most time with: *you*. You're in your own company constantly. You've been there with yourself since the beginning and will be there until the end. You've probably heard the saying, "Be your own best friend." I'd like to take that a step further and say, "Be your own best boss." Think of the greatest boss you could possibly have, one who encourages you, trusts you, gives you autonomy, can see your potential, pulls you up to a higher standard, is keenly aware of your timeframes and helps keep you on schedule. Your own best boss is fair and kind and accepts no excuses.

How can people become their own success story?

Success is a feeling. If you asked everyone what success means to them, you would get different answers. The dictionary definition is *the favourable or prosperous termination of attempts or endeavours; the accomplishment of one's goals*. To me this means that success is relative uniquely to you and your goals.

A Creative Mind

As you're reading this now, you may not realise what a great achievement that is. I could barely read a sentence until I was an adult in my twenties. I'm dyslexic, and this went undiagnosed until I was twenty-two.

When I look at words, they move around the page and sometimes disappear altogether or appear somewhere else. The letters on the page vibrate, sometimes so much they blur indistinguishably. Dyslexics don't see the words as flat on the page, but rather in 3D.

You might think dyslexia is a terrible thing, but I don't. I wouldn't change it for anything. The upside is that because I see in 3D, my brain has been taught to see and experience multiple perspectives, not just in the visual sense but in others as well. Working as a coach gives me an incredibly valuable edge. I see every side of my clients' challenges and am able to give them more insight than someone who just sees in 2D. This has created a unique and effective way of facilitating change and healing.

Dyslexic people are highly intelligent. Perhaps this is because we have to work so hard and use multiple parts of the brain. This knowledge helped me discard the childhood years of routinely being told I was of low intelligence and wouldn't amount to anything.

It was hard for me to learn to read, so I highly value this skill and have enormous gratitude for it.

Think about the greatest challenges you've overcome in your life. There's always an upside to every challenge you face, even the most traumatic experiences, and you need to search until you find it. Write down your challenges, contemplate them, own and revel in them, and don't give up until you're grateful for the lessons you've learnt. This is the greatest success.

Elissa Freeman

The past is over. Be grateful for the empowering lessons you've learnt from each event. I know this can be difficult in the beginning, but you can find the empowering lessons if you work at it.

 To discover more about how Elissa can help you *Elevate Your Mindset*, simply visit www.elevatebooks.com/mindset

Shirley Jane Jackson
Mindset and Wellness

Shirley Jane Jackson is an international author, motivational keynote speaker, empowerment coach and consultant.

After being seriously injured, Shirley became determined to make a positive difference by empowering others to overcome adversity and reach their personal victory, while inspiring them to discover their innate abilities. She seeks to make learning engaging, fun, achievable and measurable.

Shirley exudes energy and a zest for life that transfers to all she meets. At a time when many of her peers are settling down for retirement, she's embarking on a motivational authoring, speaking and coaching journey. It's her mission to deliver hope to those still questioning life and help them to thrive as they transition into the Age of Technology.

Shirley Jane Jackson
Mindset and Wellness

What is your biggest life lesson?

It's taken me sixty-two of my sixty-four years to realise that love and trust come from within me.

I would say I've spent most of my life looking for external approval. Seeking love as an external expression, rather than knowing, loving, trusting and valuing myself as I now do.

I know I've missed some important lessons, where situations might have turned out quite differently had I trusted in my own intuition.

What does love mean to you?

The essence of true love comes from going deep within myself to a huge, beautiful and infinite space within me. It's hard to find the words to define that space, but I know with every ounce of my being that it doesn't have a roof or a basement. There are no sides. It's just space. And when I close my eyes and breathe into that space, I feel the absolute essence of sheer, crystal white light. Being aware that I'm infinite in my capacity is spiritual, it's emotional and it makes me tingle all over. I'm just now tapping into this most amazing source.

What would you like your legacy to be?

To create an endless source of income and abundance for the universe. Legacy has become really important to me. It's helped me rebuild my self-esteem, find my love and heal myself. If I can reach a point of healing through the capacity of mindset at this stage of my life, I'm going to move and shake and create this abundant stream, so I can be a beneficence, for lack of a better word.

What is the message you would like to share with the world?

Somehow, a sector of our society remains marginalised. From personal experience, I would define marginalised people as those who are misunderstood by society and often suffer mental health issues. They've had various diagnoses that amount to nothing more than a label that's been hung on them.

I don't believe life is fair, but it doesn't have to be. Everyone just needs to find a way to cope with adversities.

I can be quite contentious in my opinions and attitudes. However, growing up as the youngest of seven kids, as well as having parents recovering from the great depression, I know what it's like to have a poverty of mindset, love, and spirit.

I've lived my entire life in this space, and when I talk about marginalised people, I think I do so with a degree of authority. When I attended Flinders University, South Australia to do my Bachelor of Nursing, I was invited to be a tutor at university hall. I had three-hundred bright, energetic thriving minds in my hands, and when I reflect on that I'm totally blown away to think, *How on earth could Shirley Jane Jackson have been given this enormous responsibility?*

I had my own study to accomplish, as well. I'd been studying health sciences and nursing while associating with some of the brightest minds who are now serving our community, in all forms of sciences, and making a huge difference in our world.

If I could hold those people in the palm of my hand, they'd be tiny little crystal bubbles, so fragile and yet united in strength, with an endless capacity for responsibility. One of my favourite sayings is, "To whom much is given, from him much is expected" (Luke 12:48).

Shirley Jane Jackson

As I reflect, I have to wonder where these three-hundred people are now, in terms of their influence in the huge global universe. What corners are they in? Where are they serving? Are they driving and influencing science? Are they bounding around the world? Are they living lives of freedom, joy and prosperity?

This leaves me with a huge sense of awe. What a privilege it was to have been their house mum, their mentor and their tutor.

I did some elementary psychology in my studies as part of my nursing degree, and I was also well trained by Flinders for the responsibility. I will always be truly grateful for this.

Little did I know that twenty years later, my true enlightening and wakeup time would occur, as I'm now an author at age sixty-four.

What is your big WHY?

I truly believe that education is an empowerment process. My future legacy will be known as the Andrew Charles Jackson Memorial Trust Fund. I came up with that name to honour the children I've lost in my life, and Andrew, who died at fifteen months.

My marginalised people deserve to be loved and receive an education. It only takes baby steps. The pathway to love, I believe, is a simple one. I'll *shout* it from the rooftops: education equals empowerment!

Empowerment attracts the marginalised, and my mission is to set the captives free.

What is your life purpose?

I dropped out from school during year ten, following a car accident. All I ever wanted was to become a nurse. Because I grew up with a dad who suffered with cancer for twenty years, the only life I knew was caring for others' needs. Back then, my purpose was helping to

Mindset and Wellness

meet those needs while surrounded by a large family, with everyone contributing.

We survived as welfare recipients, which always made me feel less than my peers. I knew my family was judged, pitied and known as the "poor" people down the street.

Thirty-plus years later, in the peak of my career while working in Central Australia, I experienced a serious injury in the workplace.

That's when I hit my rock bottom and became trapped in my circumstances, living in incredible physical and emotional pain. My entire life had caught up with me.

But with hindsight, I realise it put me in a position to be an advocate for others and lead them to find their own innate power.

I've always been in positions of leadership, from class captain to team leader of the St. John Ambulance Volunteers. In the eighties I was a partner in a business that was acknowledged as a Telstra Small Business Award Winner in South Australia and Nationally. Due to a good foundation, this company still runs today.

I've considered myself a slow learner. However, I'm now able to understand that my colourful life has been rich with lessons. I needed to become my own healer. To go deep within and seek the lessons.

I believe I'm being called to be a source of creativity and to reach out with both hindsight and insight. My purpose has become empowering people to continue their education and to let them know that giving up is never an option.

I want to empower others to overcome adversity and reach their personal victory. I want to invoke fun and inspiration to learn, regardless of age or ethnicity.

Shirley Jane Jackson

Learning needs to be engaging, fun, achievable and measurable.

My mission is to remain aware of ways I can influence change to bring improved outcomes for the marginalised members of society and elevate them. Finding ways to do this is so important to building self-esteem in individuals who've experienced having their life squeezed out of them. I believe it's everyone's birthright to live a life of health, freedom, fun and enjoyment and to create roadways that will allow them to access what some see as belonging to a privileged few.

I believe we live in abundant times, and I'm truly excited for my adult children and grandchildren. I have every confidence they will find their way forward.

I aim every day to lead, do and inspire. If I reach one person who's suffering, then I'll consider my job fulfilled.

By assisting and facilitating change, I can help people define their purpose and enable them to move into a space of peace and fulfilment.

I'm now a part of the life source, which is made up of an abundant stream of other motivators and influences I've allowed to come into my life. These people have made a huge contribution, in a practical way, for me to discover my purpose.

How has modern technology changed the world?

Technology has changed and advanced. Now, people can listen to music wherever they go and have access to knowledge at their fingertips. They can communicate with other countries with ease and learn about different cultures. I'm so thankful that these improvements are unstoppable. I just love, as an older person, being caught up in this beautiful, energetic flow of what brings healing and abundance into people's lives.

Mindset and Wellness

What are you passionate about?

I'm passionate about delivering my message.

My purpose is to give others hope, regardless of their age; whether they're a young kid without a buck in their pocket or roof over their head, hopeless and despairing, or at the other end of the spectrum, still struggling and being defined by their need to be a recipient of social security, the Australian Pension, or Australian Disability Pension.

Don't get me wrong. I believe social security is a sign of a buoyant, abundant and compassionate society. People need time to heal.

But from personal experience, I can tell you that receiving it can make you feel degraded and disempowered, which is in direct contradiction to what I've found to be the flow of life and its energies, and living in an abundant way.

What do you think people's biggest life issues are?

People tend to judge others in terms of age and appearance.

I don't see wrinkles, bodies, shapes or colour. I do soul work. This connection comes from looking somebody in the eyes. I don't even connect to the face, which is why I don't necessarily recognise people the next time I see them.

My life has changed so much. At one time, I would have said that if something looked nice, so be it.

In connecting with people, I feel their vibration and then decide if they're someone I want to hang out with. Whether individuals are fashionable or maybe unkempt, who am I to judge them? I'm just another soul on a journey. I'm here with my mission and purpose to inspire, do, and succeed, and to love in the essence of divine respect for others.

Benjamin J Harvey, and other great mentors such as Tony Robbins and Dr John Demartini, will say you're most like the people you hang out with.

To some, for a poor person to go and hang out with wealthy people, seems totally absurd. Well last year I did exactly that. I elected to do another educational process called *The Way of the Wealthy*.

I was curious. It hasn't been part of my life experience to hang out with authentically wealthy people. I would say Australians are tight lipped around their wealth generation strategies.

This was a defining moment in my life that made it perfectly clear to me that I was closer to achieving everything I could ever have hoped for in my life. These people were transparent, empowering and gave impeccable information regarding wealth creation strategies beyond my wildest dreams.

What's the best way to help people you would class as marginalised?

I believe the best way that I can contribute is to design a fun and engaging environment and provide education that will harness and engage brain function, in order to eliminate fear, judgement and shame about past experiences. I want to bring people into their present moment and give them permission and space to create their own dreams, outcomes and lives. And if that means healing physically, then so be it.

I believe with every ounce of my being in *By the grace of God go I*, and that everyone needs to have a sense of belonging to something bigger or greater than themselves.

I have an alignment with other people who have different belief mechanisms, and though I understand there's a greatness bigger than what I can possibly imagine, at the same time I would say that I've evolved and developed a deeper sense of spirituality.

Mindset and Wellness

It's that sense of ultimate belief that I like to introduce in my programs, as I assist others in creating healthy attitudes and help them to know it's safe to engage and accept new possibilities.

I think the biggest mistake people make, and perhaps what holds them back from thriving, is having a small world view. In my opinion, your higher power doesn't want you to be small. Humility is a beautiful thing, but you shouldn't have to shy away or hide. Appreciating the blessing of life, and connecting with a higher power, comes with a great sense of responsibility.

The brain is an absolute infinite source of possibility. There's no way it will ever run out. And if you have a brain injury, or in my case, twelve points of spinal cord injury, you need to harness what you have. Tap into the source of your own greatness and sense of genius.

For instance, I've never enjoyed reading. At university I held a fluoro yellow highlighter in my hand and highlighted everything. I didn't know until recently I'd been living with significant cataracts for a period of time that really obscured my world view. Now that the cataracts are gone, there's no stopping me.

I believe everyone can be another Florey, Einstein or any of the other greatest minds of the world. It could be you. It might be me. I don't know. But I've had the enormous opportunity to reflect on this through years of adversity to get to this point.

How are mindset and wellness connected?

You might be wondering where you should go from here in applying mindset to wellness.

I've come to truly value my mindset, and I could never be unaware of it again. It's given me structure and strategy and has assisted me in rearranging my thinking. Mindset gives me peace, love and enjoyment in my life. Every day as I wake, the first thing I'm consciously aware of is that I'm breathing. I allow that air to come in, permeate into my body and feed my cells as quickly as possible. A new day has broken, and with it brings a new opportunity to live in the moment and ask myself, *What else can I do? What else can I be today?*

Everyone has the same twenty-four hours, and if you go looking for tomorrow on a calendar, you won't find it. All you have is this day and whatever you choose to do with it. Maximize the opportunity. Breathe it in, while having a conscious awareness of it. Don't allow your hindbrain to remain in a lull, just soaking and mopping up everything subliminally. Allowing some of that greatness and energy to transfer into your forebrain can be a truly exciting experience.

You talk about the hindbrain and the forebrain. Can you explain further?

I'd like you to think about the brain being in three spaces. To keep it simple I will use terms like forebrain, midbrain, and hindbrain. The forebrain regulates intuitive functions like temperature, reproductive functions, eating, sleeping and the display of emotion. The midbrain relays information between the hindbrain and the forebrain, particularly information coming from the eyes and the ears. The hindbrain includes the medulla, which is responsible for controlling breathing, regulating reflexes, and maintaining your posture, the cerebellum, which is responsible for coordinating motor activity, and the pons that serves as the bridge towards the midbrain and is responsible for monitoring sleep and arousal.

I've discovered through the teachings of Benjamin J. Harvey that it's possible to use various techniques to intercept these neural pathway junctions and create new pathways.

Mindset and Wellness

The majority of the time the forebrain exists in a space of just kind of being there, and unless you invite it to play it's not going to do anything, so the hindbrain will take over. Now, for some people this is fine, but for others who may have experienced compounded trauma or compounded events, especially in regard to grief, there will be major obstacles to reaching the abundant and beautiful life you were born to have.

To be in a state of gratitude, you need to become unshackled from the hindbrain. If you picture the weight of a human body being totally wrapped in chains, once you find the key and open them, it will give you the power and permission to be able to engage with full consciousness.

Have you had any aha moments that changed your life?

I knew I had a deep passion, but it was like I was trapped inside of myself, and I just never knew how to express that.

I recently had a cat that ironically died on my father's birthday. He passed away back in 1968, when I was only thirteen. Before that, he'd had a twenty-year battle with cancer, so my memory consists of growing up in illness, with morphine syringes rattling around in a saucepan and a very sick daddy.

The earlier years, before he got sick, Dad abused me both sexually and emotionally. I had six other siblings, and we were all distressed and distraught from our early childhood upbringing. Don't get me wrong. I'm totally healed from that situation. I love my family, even my dad, who I learned later in life had four mums by the time he was twelve and ran away from home.

I started doing nursing at sixteen, and on my first day there were four deaths, along with the loss of my father and grandfather, who'd lived with us. But I experienced loss and grief in a family unable to express their emotions. They sent me away, so I wasn't involved in the grieving processes, which means when I was just a young girl, I learnt the coping strategy of bottling things up.

By the time I was nineteen I had my first child, who was born with cerebral palsy. To say this was distressing and perplexing is an understatement, especially since it was the seventies, and there was little known at the time about how to deal with a profoundly brain damaged child. He had no sight and could barely function, and he died at fifteen months.

The grief and pain were devastating, particularly for myself. All I knew was just love, love, love, and all of a sudden, I didn't have that baby to love anymore. It crippled me emotionally.

By the time I was twenty-nine, I'd birthed eight children, five of whom didn't survive. I needed emotional support, so I headed down the path of having psychiatry, psychology, and counsellors enter my life. After forty-two years of continuous therapy, I never found any of it assistive, but somehow the outside world expected me to steely myself. I was told, "Come on, it's not much good to be crying", "You don't really need to go there, it's over", "Let's move on", and "Looking back isn't going to be very helpful."

In terms of my self-esteem, after achieving so much in my life, having to step down after my work injury had a huge impact on me. I was absolutely devastated and suffering from deep depression. Plus, due to the trauma of the memories related to it, I spent six and a half years addicted to morphine and other medications that had been prescribed for my pain management.

I lost the new momentum I'd gained after achieving my Bachelor of Nursing Degree, as well as a semester of midwifery and honours studies. I was also dealing with relationships, family and all of the stuff that happens to everyone throughout their life. There I was, in pain, in a remote part of central Australia.

Mindset and Wellness

Little did I know what WorkCover arrangement would do to me as a person. Imagine you're on a career path of brilliance, you're totally passionate about what you're doing, you're living in the moment, extraordinary opportunities are abounding, and you kind of think you have it made. Then, with one collapse, it all ends.

Somehow all of the early childhood programming that had established my brain health and wellness, didn't support me during this time. I had nothing to really grab hold of. It's one thing to have your affairs in place, but it's another to emotionally reach a state where your brain isn't functioning at capacity, and you can only deal with what you know.

On 12 March 2016, I attended a seminar called Prosper from your Passion. It was run by the co-directors of Authentic Education in Sydney, Benjamin J Harvey and Cham Tang. Till the day my work is done, I will never be able to thank these young men enough for their motivation, inspiration and passing the baton of will to me. Up to that point in time, I didn't care whether I lived or died. I felt I was on a scrap heap; my education had been taken from me, and the disempowering process around insurers, WorkCover, and my situation, was totally deplorable.

With the seminar taking place the same day as my mother's birthday, I felt a really strong sense that she thought it would be a great idea for me. I suppose there was a degree of escapism to get away from the pain and trauma of my compounded loss, though I wasn't in touch with that at the time.

My injury occurred in April 2008, so by the time I was in that conference, I'd had over seven years of multiple surgeries and injuries and spent a period of time on a disability pension, living in a housing trust unit. I'd had two unsuccessful complete knee replacements and was in terrible physical pain.

I would say within the first three hours I was totally riveted and engaged in something that was quite new to me. Prior to this day, I'd spent forty-four years as a seriously depressed person and carried many diagnoses, including major depression syndrome and borderline personality. I'd had four hospital admissions and a mandatory detention. I also suffered from Post-Traumatic Stress Disorder as a result of my work in central Australia as a remote area nurse.

When I heard Benjamin Harvey say, "Dream your wildest dreams. Unleash that grandiosity that's inside of you. Do what you want to do. Find what you love. Love what you do", it blew me away and helped me further engage in the process of personal and professional development.

It was like someone turned a key inside of me, unleashing all of the traumatic events in my life, and I was able to rapidly place the jigsaw puzzle pieces of myself together.

I think what happened to me on 12 March 2016, was that I was thrown a key to unlock this person living her life in a marginalised way.

Since that time, I've been travelling in my wheelchair to the east coast of Australia and within South Australia, so I can soak up as much inspiring professional development as I can and continue to apply daily processes to my life and circumstances. But wherever I'm travelling, I'm usually plugged in.

I've achieved much in my life and had many accomplishments along the way, which is kind of sweet, because I understand so much more now than I did then. At the time I couldn't quite get it. But now I think, *Yes, thank you. I'm blessed. I understand I have a job to do.* I believe that job is to inspire, do, and lead others. I want to help them have a sense of accomplishment and the feeling of achieving a life well-lived.

So, if I didn't actually have the injury, I wouldn't be here, talking to you about mindset and how I managed to muster resilience from within myself that I didn't even know I had.

Due to immersing myself in continuous professional development, for the first time in my life I've had the functionality of the brain explained to me. Even throughout my nursing curriculum that included anatomy and physiology, as well as my own research and studies, I'd never actually had these aspects explained in a way that I could apply them to my own lack of wellbeing and negative thought processes.

Mindset has provided me a different toolkit after many, many years of psychology and psychotherapy.

I've gained an understanding of my early childhood development and other experiences of my life and how they've really been positioned in my hindbrain, flickering around the entire time and holding tremendous capacity to influence how I acted out or survived.

How are you currently making a difference?

Mostly by paying it forward. I lead by example and try to exemplify the changes I'm applying to my life. Taking responsibility for me, and creating my outcomes, has to ultimately make a difference in my life and the lives of those around me. I see all of my relationships changing, evolving and flourishing by sharing my *Emotional Freedom Coaching* techniques.

I'm proactive in speaking out for social truth and dignity for those with disabilities. I call out for accountability from policy and decision makers to develop consciousness and awareness, such as making improvements to buildings that don't have facilities for those who use a wheelchair, so they're able to fully experience life.

My goal is to continue my education and become an author, speaker and coach.

Having experienced a life sprinkled with adversity, I love to elevate others and assist them to shine. To do this, I've been running a meet-up group in Adelaide for small business owners and entrepreneurs. It's open to anyone. As the saying goes, "Creativity is contagious. Pass it on."

I want to take someone's hand and lead them from a path of poverty to a life of abundance, which doesn't necessarily mean being rich, although money is a good and beautiful exchange for value received.

We are living in exciting times. Who said you have to retire and be a pensioner at age sixty-five? If you have your health and mindset geared toward ageing healthily, and continue to educate yourself about the aging process, you can stay motivated and socially interactive.

Everyone knows activity directly impacts your thinking. My experience tells me that mindset is the major determining factor towards wellness and ageing.

Now at peace, I feel proud that my world is a happy place.

 To discover more about how Shirley can help you *Elevate Your Mindset*, simply visit www.elevatebooks.com/mindset

Aldwyn Altuney

Inspiring Good News

Aldwyn Altuney, known as the Media Queen, is a photojournalist with thirty-four years of experience in TV, radio, print and online media.

She hosts online TV shows, the Techwebcast podcast and workshops on How to Gain $1M Worth of Free Publicity.

Born in Sydney and based on the Gold Coast, Aldwyn runs AA Xposé Media, which offers public relations packages and the Mass Media Mastery program.

Passionate about the humane treatment of animals, Aldwyn founded the world's first Animal Action Day in 2007, for which she has raised millions of dollars in free media exposure. She also started a global Good News Day on August 8, 2018.

Connect with Aldwyn on Facebook, Twitter, Google+, LinkedIn, Instagram, Pinterest, YouTube and www.aaxpose.com.

Aldwyn Altuney

Inspiring Good News

What is your big WHY?

I'm passionate about inspiring a positive world where people love what they do, are excited about living life to their full potential and making a difference to the world around them. I'm an advocate for people having compassion for themselves and others, speaking their truth and choosing love over fear as they speak up for what they truly believe in.

I envisage a world where more positive stories are being reported than negative ones, helping to decrease depression and suicide rates.

I'm also passionate about inspiring action for the humane treatment of animals.

What message do you wish to share with the world?

I want people to understand and appreciate the miracle they are as human beings. Every person has a unique gift and message to bring to the world.

Just by being born, they've beaten about one billion other swimmers to the finish line.

The few who run the world want people to live a small life and be a slave to the system. The mainstream education and political system is brainwashing them. Most are completely oblivious to it.

Those who are aware are combining forces to affect positive change in the world and wake people up, particularly in the areas of health, peace, sustainability and environmental protection.

You can create a ripple effect of change by being courageous and speaking your truth.

What decisions have you made that changed your life?

I've made quite a few decisions that have changed my life and, in some cases, saved it.

I believe there are no mistakes and that everything happens for a reason. I have no regrets about any action I've taken in my lifetime, as they've all brought me to where I am now.

Sometimes, people are blessed and have so much to be grateful for, yet they don't see it. Instead, they focus their energy on what they don't like or are not happy with, so they tend to attract more of that and wonder why they aren't given more to be thankful for.

The most powerful place to stand is taking one hundred per cent responsibility for everything that happens in your life.

I grew up in a loving household where my parents went above and beyond to ensure my brother and I had a great life. I'm of Greek, Turkish and Ukrainian heritage. Since all three countries were at war with each other, I call myself the 'love child'.

I was born in Sydney and was bullied at North Balgowlah Public School from the age of six. Fellow students would pick on me about my name, the food I ate and the clothes I wore. Anything they could pick on, they did. As such, I grew up angry at the world and started rebelling from a young age.

I was running away from home at age thirteen. At fifteen, my dad kicked me out of the house. One night, fed up with my constant rebellion to his strict rules, he said: "You're not my daughter anymore."

Aldwyn Altuney

I then moved into a crazy household in Manly with a drug-addicted drummer I was dating, his alcoholic mother and drug-dealing sister. I worked two part-time jobs to cover the rent on my shared room of $50 per week, while attending Year 11 at Mosman High School in Sydney.

This was a complete party house with non-stop music and jamming until sunrise each morning. After six months of this, there came a turning point.

When I was sixteen years old, I witnessed my best friend sleeping with my boyfriend in our bed. I can remember The Pretenders song, 'Don't Get Me Wrong', played on the turntable. I bawled my eyes out.

Soon afterwards, I called my mum in tears and said: "I can't handle this anymore."

She said to come home. Even though my dad wasn't happy about it, he gave his consent.

I'd gone from Dux of North Balgowlah Primary School in 1985 to failing everything in Year 11. I changed schools to Forest High School for Year 12 and studied hard with my brother to improve my grades.

This was a major turning point for me. After changing my environment, I discovered the grass isn't always greener on the other side and started to appreciate my parents and family so much more.

At the end of Year 12, I qualified to do a Bachelor of Arts in Communication (Media) at the University of Canberra.

While there, I applied three times to become editor of the university newspaper, *Curio*, before I was accepted. I took the fortnightly publication from twenty-four pages to forty-eight, co-ordinated thirty contributors and became the longest-serving editor at the paper. It was through this job that I discovered how much I loved the power of the media to affect change in the community.

One of the first stories I wrote was an anti duck shooting story with the headline 'Go and Get Ducked!' about people shooting ducks for fun, which I couldn't believe was legal in Australia.

This was the beginning of what soon became a lucrative career in the media.

I graduated with High Distinctions in my majors of TV Production and Photojournalism and went on to work as a journalist on TV, in radio and print media across Australia and internationally.

What are you grateful for?

There's so much I am grateful for. My loving parents and family, my friends, my health and having a fully functioning body, as well as all the travel I've done, my mentors, coaches and clients.

Whenever I find myself complaining about something or feeling like I'm falling into a dark space, I think of Nick Vujicic, a Serbian-Australian Christian evangelist and motivational speaker born without arms and legs. He's one of the seven known surviving people worldwide who live with Tetra-amelia syndrome.

After a childhood of bullying and thoughts of suicide, he's now one of the best motivational speakers around. He's also married and has two children, who have all of their limbs.

What's the best business advice you've ever received?

When I was working as a sub editor/ journalist at the *Gold Coast Sun* in 2005, I attended an event with the National College of Business.

The director, Jon Mailer, asked the crowd how much they could earn using their body from the head down. People were throwing out figures like $2000 and below. But when he asked how much they could earn working from the head up, everyone agreed the amount was endless.

He then asked if it made sense to invest ten per cent of our income in personal development. I thought it did, so that year I invested $7000 in my first personal development course, since an Alpha program I did with my family as a young child in Sydney. Since then, I've invested more than $300,000 into life and business mentors, coaches and courses, which has been invaluable for my personal and professional growth.

Why have you written a book about how good news sells?

I wrote my book, *Good News Sells—How to Gain $1M Worth of Positive Publicity*, because people don't buy into the old adage that 'bad news sells' anymore. People want more good news stories.

Most people I speak to say they don't watch the news anymore. It's too negative and depresses them.

Many headline news stories are negative and depressing, yet there is so much good happening in the world. What you see and hear, you start to believe. This means it's very important that we feed our minds with good news.

Positive media can instil hope and uplift people to create a happier and more peaceful world.

While I mostly appear to be outgoing and happy, that hasn't always been the case. I've had depression over the years and still go to some dark places occasionally. However, due to all the personal development work I've done, I don't stay there for long anymore.

In the past, I would get depressed watching the news or hearing about wars, famines, droughts and crime.

I've also had three friends take their own lives due to depression, which has been absolutely tragic and devastating for me. They had no idea how much they were loved or the impact they made in the world.

Inspiring Good News

According to the Beyond Blue support service, about one million Australian adults have depression, over two million have anxiety and forty-five per cent will experience a mental health condition in their lifetime.

According to the World Health Organisation, nearly one million people commit suicide each year worldwide, which is about one death every forty seconds or 3000 per day. For each person who takes their own life, at least twenty make an attempt. Suicide has a global mortality rate of 16 per 100,000 people.

I aim to reduce these shocking statistics using the power of positive media messages and lift spirits worldwide by encouraging people to share good news stories in social and traditional media.

I have set up a global Good News Day on August 8, 2018, to inspire people across the world to share positive news on their social media, online news channels, podcasts and in mainstream media (on TV, radio, print).

I believe it is crucial for people to share good news with themselves and others if we want to see a more peaceful, harmonious planet with people loving their lives and being kind to each other.

Number 8 is significant for several reasons. It is a lucky number in China that symbolizes prosperity, abundance, power, harmony and balance.

My good news on August 8, 2008, was that my niece Mattea was born in Gosford, New South Wales (NSW), on that day. Good News Day in 2018 marks her 10th birthday.

Ideally, I would like every day to be Good News Day and encourage people regularly to share on social media what their good news is for that day.

Aldwyn Altuney

What's the worst thing that ever happened to you? How did you overcome it?

I've had a few near-death experiences in my life, including having a quinsy in my throat on New Year's Eve in 2014. My condition flared after I emceed for Colin Hay, lead vocalist of Men at Work, at the Woodford Folk Festival on the Sunshine Coast. I ended up in the Royal Brisbane and Women's Hospital on an antibiotic drip for three days.

A quinsy, also known as a peritonsillar abscess, is a rare and potentially serious complication of tonsillitis, which can kill you in a short amount of time if the swelling in the throat blocks the airway.

This experience made me appreciate my life like never before. Hundreds of Facebook messages of support came through, which brought many tears of gratitude for all the amazing people in my life.

It also made me wonder who would show up for my funeral if I died, what kind of legacy I would leave and what I wanted to create for my life. I often ask myself these questions when I set goals or contemplate the future.

What's one of the most shocking things that's ever happened to you?

When I first moved to the Gold Coast in January 2000, I never planned to stay there. My goal was always to live in America, so I rented apartments for the first two years.

In 2002, I had to move from my unit in Labrador, as the owner wanted the place for her daughter to live. Since I was a busy journalist at the time, I decided to put an ad in the *Gold Coast Bulletin* inquiring if anyone had a suitable place for me to rent.

I received a call from a guy named Lee, who said he had a place in Main Beach across from the ocean, which sounded perfect, so I popped in to see the apartment.

When I arrived, I found out Lee was a guy in his early twenties and looked like a surfy dude. His young eighteen-year-old girlfriend was pregnant and lying on the bed.

I gave him about $1000 in rent and bond, which was more than my weekly wage back then. He gave me the keys.

When I later went back to the apartment, there was rubbish all over the floor, as well as rotten eggs and food in the sink. Also, the door to the balcony wouldn't close.

I suddenly had this sinking feeling in my stomach, so I asked the people in the apartment next door if they knew whether the previous tenants were going to clean the apartment. They suggested I speak to the manager.

When I did, I was told that Lee did not own the apartment and owed three weeks of rent! We were both furious. I gave the manager the keys and cried for about a week. I couldn't believe someone would do that. And even though police closed the case, I never received any money back.

That's when I decided I would never rent again and bought a house in Southport. Now, sixteen years on, I've fully renovated the house and still live there. I may have lost $1000, but I'd make more than $100,000 if I sold my house today.

I also believe in karma. What comes around goes around ten-fold and not necessarily by the same people you rip off or do wrong or right to.

Aldwyn Altuney

What achievements are you most proud of?

One of my highest achievements was in table tennis. I beat the number thirty-two in the world, Alexandra Brusnado, at the Italian Open Championships in 1990, when I was sixteen.

I was named 2005 Climber of the Year at the National College of Business Gala Awards night and was a Community Award finalist for two years with the Women in Business Awards in 2014 and 2015.

I've won several Humorous Speech contests with Toastmasters International and graduated with a PHD Certification from Authentic Education.

One of the achievements I'm most proud of is creating Animal Action events to increase awareness, appreciation and respect for all animals.

When people understand how important it is to treat animals better, they become aware of the need to treat themselves and others better, which creates a more peaceful and harmonious world for everyone.

To date, I've run eleven annual Animal Action events on the Gold Coast since 2007 and raised over $20,000 for various animal charities, as well as millions of dollars of free media exposure for the humane treatment of animals worldwide.

With my media work, I inspire people to recognise they're a miracle, to have an appreciation for their unique gifts and to speak up about what they're passionate about.

How did you become interested in the media? Also, what experiences have you had in relation to it?

My fascination with the media began at age ten when *The Manly Daily*, in Sydney's northern beaches, interviewed me for table tennis. I was the number-one ranked Australian junior table tennis player in the under fifteen and under seventeen girls' divisions at the time.

The photographer was doing a shoot from the top of a ladder, looking down at me with a bat and ball in hand at the table in the family garage. That's when I thought, *Wow, that's really creative. I'd love to do something like that one day.*

I went on to appear on *Agro's Cartoon Connection* at age eleven with my brother Nicholas. He was also a top junior table tennis player in NSW and now runs his own optometry business, Eyes by Design, in Gosford.

I received my first TV presentation/ interview skills training that year during a camp with other elite junior athletes, sponsored by MLC Junior Sports Foundation. This was alongside the likes of TV presenter/ former competitive swimmer Johanna Griggs, whose mother was my Grade 6 teacher at North Balgowlah Public School.

At age thirteen, I started my own radio show at Radio Manly Warringah.

At age sixteen, I did work experience as a Journalist with *The Manly Daily*.

While at the University of Canberra, I co-wrote, directed and produced the short film, *Batteries Not Included*, which won Best Film among sixty fellow media students.

I've worked as an editor, sub editor, journalist, photographer and graphic designer on various publications.

I've also been a freelance writer for interstate and national magazines, as well as a columnist, radio host and actress/ producer in short films and TV, including commercials.

Aldwyn Altuney

After years of working in the fast-paced media industry, I thought, *Why don't I just do this for myself?* So I started my own business, *AA Xposé Photography*, in 2002 while working as a journalist at the *Gold Coast Sun*.

What is your business?

When I left the *Gold Coast Sun* in 2005, my business evolved into *AA Xposé Media*, as people also began requesting PR work, copywriting, video and graphic design.

I did my first media training workshops in 2003 and had repeated calls for more.

In 2014, I launched a media-training program called Mass Media Mastery, where I teach people how to gain free publicity. I now have clients from all over Australia, the UK, Netherlands, South Africa and New Zealand. Most of them are small business people, authors and speakers I've never met. Such is the power of online marketing.

In a nutshell, I help people propel their message, product or service to the masses, so they can build their credibility and profile in the community, profit in their business and leave a legacy.

What makes you or your business stand out from your competitors?

What makes my business stand out is the variety of media I've worked in behind the scenes and running the only media company I know of that guarantees media exposure with our PR packages.

I also have a huge heart for all living beings and a strong community focus.

What are some of your life highlights?

As a photojournalist working in the media and in my business, I've covered some amazing national and international events and interviewed stars including Hugh Jackman, Cyndi Lauper and Russell Crowe. There's never a dull moment with what I do.

Nowadays, I also run Media Blitz and Mass Media Mastery Workshops for authors, speakers, small business people and social entrepreneurs. In 2018, I launched a Meetup group called Mass Media Masters.

What's the biggest mistake people make when approaching the media for free publicity?

They approach the media with an angle that's too commercial and not newsworthy. The story needs to be something of interest to the wider population and not just to sell a new product or service.

The newsworthy angle is often found in the story behind the product, service or person being promoted, or how they help people with what they do.

What is your system to gain free publicity?

In my Mass Media Mastery program, I cover the 5 Power Steps to gaining one million dollars' worth of free publicity. These are:

▶ **Step 1: Perfect angle**

   I have a system called BAM:

   - Brainstorm: Know what angle(s) to pitch to the media.

   - Analyse: What's newsworthy about you or your business?

   - Message: What's unique or different about your business? What valuable information can you offer readers, listeners or viewers?

▶ **Step 2: Organise a campaign**

Once you know the angle you're going to promote to the media, you will need a press kit or a simplified press release and/ or promotional photos.

The press release needs to fit on one page (300-500 words) and answer the five W's and H (who, what, where, when, why and how). Your photos need to be relevant and in several formats (vertical and horizontal, high resolution and 300 dpi jpg).

Once you have your press release and photos media ready, you need to send them out to relevant media outlets and online PR sites. You can also have a PR representative do this for you, which is a better choice, as it always looks better coming from a third party.

Next, make the most of the main social media sites and blast a snippet of your story on Facebook, Twitter, LinkedIn, Google+, Pinterest and Instagram.

▶ **Step 3: WOW the media**

This step is all about wowing the media, like 'stunt king' Richard Branson (of Virgin fame) does.

As the media think in images, visuals are extremely important to the success of your PR campaign.

▶ **Step 4: Embrace your message**

You need to prepare for interviews and aim to inspire people with your message. I suggest you have three main points front of mind, do mock interviews, video yourself and play it back. Then review for improvement.

▸ **Step 5: Reap rewards**

The fortune is in the follow up. This can be done by phone or email with specific media.

I suggest having a spreadsheet or other system for tracking responses. Outline the date, time, contact person's details and action steps after all communication. Make sure you take action in a timely and appropriate manner.

Once your story has appeared in print or been aired on radio or TV, obtain the press clippings, mp3s or video clips/ links. Then blast these on your social media, as well as your website.

Note: Before posting anything on social media, always check any copyright restrictions.

What are some of your most inspiring client stories?

I did a media campaign to help launch Australia's largest online shopping mall, *Aussie Mega Mall*, in 2016.

I helped gain them Channel 7 and 9 TV exposure, as well as feature stories in *Australian Giftguide*, *Power Retail*, *CEO* and *Artinzene* magazines, interviews on the *Media Mastery Show* and *Techwebcast* podcast, among others.

Since the launch on the Gold Coast with 3500 merchants, the Australian startup has grown to over 32,000 Australian online stores collectively showcasing more than two million products in 2018.

The company has now launched the UK Mega Mall and is about to launch the US and NZ Mega Malls. It is now the 'Uber of online shopping', worth more than two million dollars locally and potentially the next billion dollar global brand.

I also worked with 'Webinar Guy' Steven Essa to promote his national Web Business Breakthrough event in Australia and New Zealand.

He'd previously employed several PR people but none were able to gain him any media exposure.

After working with me for just one month, he gained over two million dollars in free publicity, including a six-minute interview on Sky News Business, a thirty-one minute radio interview on 3RRR in Melbourne that ran three times and a one-page feature story in *Vision China Times* that ran in English and Chinese.

After interviewing Steve, each of the reporters became interested in working with him as well.

In addition to gaining potential new clients in the media, he can now include *As seen on TV* in his marketing. This is invaluable for building trust and credibility in the community, particularly as reputation marketing is so important for anyone with an online business.

I also helped women's empowerment coach, Michelle Patterson, gain an exclusive two-page spread in *Woman's Day*, Australia's number one weekly magazine. After thirty years of keeping it a secret, she opened up about her secret forced adoption at age sixteen and shared her story to 1.6 million readers.

If Michelle had paid for advertising in the magazine, she would have spent $60,000. The publicity value is worth three to eight times more in credibility and is seen twenty-two times more than ads. If you average the value, this two-page spread was worth about $300,000 to her.

She can also use the *Woman's Day* logo on her website and in marketing indefinitely.

With technology and online marketing strategies changing all the time, how do you keep up?

To stay on top of my game, I go to a lot of courses in Australia and overseas, attend numerous webinars and study business, marketing and the media.

I believe in constant never-ending improvement.

What mindset do you believe is needed to create a great life?

Be courageous, remain peaceful no matter what life throws at you and have high integrity with your personal and business dealings. Speak your truth and choose love, not fear. Realise that, as David Icke says: *"You're infinite consciousness and anything is possible for you."*

How does someone keep inspired on a daily basis?

It's important to be clear on your goals and write them down. Meditate, visualise, read your goals daily and love yourself, so you can truly love others.

Eat healthy raw foods as much as possible, exercise often and do things you love. Nurture yourself mentally, physically and emotionally.

What are your favourite ways to relax and enjoy life?

I love travelling, acting, doing personal development and business seminars, exercising, performing, seeing live bands, reading, art exhibitions and creating my own artwork. I also love body surfing and indulging in massages, saunas and spas.

My appreciation for the performance arts led me to emcee one of the biggest stages at the Woodford Folk Festival for about fifteen years, working alongside many famous people, including TV hosts, comedians and singer-songwriters.

How do you make the most of your time?

The power is in the present, so being focused, disciplined and organised is crucial.

When I'm on deadline, I batch my tasks, use a timer in fifteen to ninety-minute bursts and ignore all distractions.

What do you think people's biggest challenges in life are?

I've found self-doubt and self-criticism to be some of the biggest barriers to people moving forward and achieving their goals and dreams.

What's the best way to help them with this issue?

I encourage people to choose gratitude and love.

Everyone is extraordinary. Too many people are hard on themselves. There's simply no need for it.

When you learn to love and nurture yourself physically, mentally and emotionally, you can become the best version of yourself.

I also encourage you to choose your friends and environment wisely. They say eighty per cent of your happiness comes from whom you choose as a life partner, so choose well. Don't let the weeds infiltrate your garden of life!

What can someone do now to change their life and become their own success story?

- Make healthier choices with the food you eat, movies you watch, friends you keep and activities you undertake.

- Be grateful for what you have.

- Make the most of what you've been given.

- Make peace with everyone. Resentment is like drinking poison and expecting the other person to die. Life is too short to poison yourself with negative thoughts about yourself or others.

- Learn to be your own best friend and love yourself, so you can truly love others.

- Take time out to smell the roses. Get some eco therapy. Embrace nature and the wonderful world you live in.

- Live the life of your dreams. See it, feel it and act on it. You can have anything you set your mind to so go for it!

What are some of your future goals?

I would love to have an offline TV show one day to complement my online ones on the Aldwyn Altuney YouTube channel and for my online shows to attract more than ten-million viewers worldwide, while acquiring abundant sponsors and advertisers.

I want to keep interviewing people and sharing their stories and wisdom.

My intention is for my *Good News Sells* book to be an international best-seller and to grow a global movement of more good news stories in the mass media. I believe this will make a massive difference in reducing depression and suicide rates and lift people's spirits.

Another goal is for Mass Media Mastery to be known as the best mass media training program globally and for my clients to gain media exposure worldwide, so they can make a huge impact with their service, product or message.

Aldwyn Altuney

I'd love to travel the world as a highly paid professional speaker and author, to inspire people to live their passions and take positive action for the humane treatment of animals.

Other goals are for Animal Action Events to be held regularly worldwide, to run an animal sanctuary and to have breeding programs for endangered animals.

Is there a significant quote or saying you live by?

I chose this quote for my Miss January page in the 2015 Inspiring Women's Calendar that raised money for the no-kill shelter, the Animal Welfare League of Queensland:

> "A small group of thoughtful people can change the world. Indeed, it's the only thing that ever has."
> ~ Margaret Mead.

I believe everything has a ripple effect and can make a difference. Most people just don't realise the power or impact they have.

How would you like to be remembered?

I would like people to smile when they think of me and to know that I'm someone who always spoke my truth and inspired positive change on the planet for people, animals and the environment.

I would like to be known as someone with a huge heart who inspired people to take action on their passions, step up and step out with their message and create a more compassionate and peaceful world.

What message would you like to share with the world?

Live and share your music with the world. Don't die with it in you.

Leave a legacy for your family and friends. Know that just by being alive and living life to the full, you've inspired a better and more peaceful world for future generations to come.

How can people connect with you?

Like my 'Media Queen', 'Good News Sells' and 'Mass Media Mastery' pages on Facebook, where I give regular free PR tips.

Connect with me on Facebook, Twitter, LinkedIn, G+, Pinterest, Instagram and subscribe to the 'Aldwyn Altuney' channel on YouTube.

You can also visit my AA Xposé Media website at www.aaxpose.com.

Here's to your media success. Anything is possible when you step up and step out with your message. ☺

 To discover more about how Aldwyn can help you *Elevate Your Mindset*, simply visit www.elevatebooks.com/mindset

Afterword

While you were reading these people's inspiring stories, did you notice something? All of their life experiences were for a purpose, bringing them closer to their goals, relationships and especially the message they were meant to share with the world.

The last page is a blank canvas for you to write the next chapter of your own story about elevating your mindset and inspiring others. Every day is a brand-new opportunity to be the author of your destiny.

Next Steps

To support you on your journey to *Elevate Your Mindset,* we recommend you take advantage of these resources:

7 Day Transformation Program

Learn ONE powerful 'Elevate Process' you can use immediately to improve Your Relationships, Health, Finances, Mindset and any other area of your life.

To join this 7-day transformation online program, simply go to: www.elevatebooks.com/you

👥 Connect with the Authors

To discover more about the authors and what they have to teach you, and bonus gifts they are offering visit:
www.elevatebooks.com/mindset

🎙 Subscribe to our Podcast

If you'd like to hear the go-to interviews from the authors and be re-inspired, check out: www.elevatebooks.com/podcast

🌐 Visit the Website

To find out more about the Elevate book series, visit: www.elevatebooks.com

www.ingramcontent.com/pod-product-compliance
Lightning Source LLC
Chambersburg PA
CBHW071232080526
44587CB00013BA/1588